CONTEMPORARY GERMAN PHILOSOPHY

T0370620

AN INTRODUCTION
TO
CONTEMPORARY GERMAN PHILOSOPHY

by

WERNER BROCK, Dr. PHIL.

*sometime Lecturer in Philosophy at the
University of Freiburg i. Br.*

CAMBRIDGE

AT THE UNIVERSITY PRESS

1935

CAMBRIDGE
UNIVERSITY PRESS

University Printing House, Cambridge CB2 8BS, United Kingdom

Published in the United States of America by Cambridge University Press, New York

Cambridge University Press is part of the University of Cambridge.

It furthers the University's mission by disseminating knowledge in the pursuit of
education, learning and research at the highest international levels of excellence.

www.cambridge.org
Information on this title: www.cambridge.org/9781107415973

© Cambridge University Press 1935

First published 1935
First paperback edition 2014

A catalogue record for this publication is available from the British Library

ISBN 978-1-107-41597-3 Paperback

To

MY PARENTS

CONTENTS

Foreword   *page* xi

Preface   xv

CHAPTER I

The Beginnings of Contemporary German Philosophy

1. German Humanism and the development of the
    separate sciences as the background for Con-
    temporary German Philosophy   *page* 2

2. Two new philosophical movements since Hegel:
    attempts towards a philosophical synthesis
    of scientific results; and epistemological en-
    quiries   9

3. Husserl   15

4. Dilthey   20

5. Max Weber   26

6. A third stage of post-Hegelian philosophy as
    reached by Husserl, Dilthey and Weber   40

CHAPTER II

*Nietzsche and Kierkegaard: their importance for
Contemporary German Philosophy*

1. Nietzsche's importance for Germany's intellec-
    tual life as a whole and especially for Con-
    temporary German Philosophy   46

CONTENTS

2. Nietzsche's criticism of Science   *page* 49

3. Nietzsche's conception of the Philosopher   54

4. Nietzsche's "Philosophy of Life"   62

5. Nietzsche's influence on some later thinkers: Simmel, Scheler, Spengler, Klages   67

6. Kierkegaard's personality and work   72

7. Kierkegaard's thoughts on "Choice"   78

8. Kierkegaard's conception of "Existenz" and "Existential thinking"   82

CHAPTER III

Present Day Philosophy

1. Brief survey of the continuance of academic tradition: N. Hartmann and E. Cassirer; the phenomenological school (Pfänder, Geiger, Reinach); the Dilthey school (Misch, Nohl, Spranger, Groethuysen, Freyer); the Gestalt-philosophy (Köhler, Wertheimer, Koffka); the scientific philosophy (Schlick, Carnap, Reichenbach)   87

2. Jaspers' conception of the philosophical attitude; his three ways of philosophising   95

3. Heidegger's conception of a new philosophical theme; the analysis of human existence as a preparatory explanation for the problem of being   109

CONTENTS

CONCLUSION

*The still undecided position of philosophy among
the determining factors in human life*   page 118

Bibliography

Part 1. Works of the principal philosophers
discussed   121

Part 2. Works of other post-Hegelian German
philosophers   133

Index   142

ix

FOREWORD

It is perhaps an unavoidable result of the great advance which philosophical studies are making at the present time in every civilised country, that it becomes more and more difficult to keep abreast of what is going on elsewhere than in one's own. At a moment when we are somewhat depressed by the darker side of recent events in Germany, the ostracism of some of her ablest and most rising young men in various departments of knowledge brings with it, like the proverbial "ill-wind", the opportunity of hearing at first-hand and receiving new stimulus from reports of what is being done there. This is particularly welcome in the field of philosophy where, with the exception of one or two of the more outstanding names (chiefly of writers such as Edmund Husserl and Nicolai Hartmann, some of whose works have appeared in English translations), recent German philosophy has been largely a closed book.

It was therefore a particularly happy thought on the part of London University to invite Dr Werner Brock, formerly Lecturer in the University of Freiburg im Breisgau, to give a course of lectures in English on any subject he might choose, and on his part to have chosen that of "An Introduction to Contemporary German Philosophy". Judging from his record I should say that there can be few, even in that land of proficient scholars, who are better fitted to treat of it. Owing to the freedom permitted by the German system in this respect he was able to study in the Universities of Berlin, Munich, Heidelberg, Freiburg and Göttingen between 1919 and 1928, devoting himself in the earlier years of that period to the history of culture and to medicine, in which he specialised in biology; in the later years exclusively to philosophy. He was thus brought into contact with many of the leading thinkers of his time, including Max Weber, Jaspers, Heidegger, Geiger, Misch, Schmalenbach and N. Hartmann, and had the opportunity of establishing intimate personal relations with most of them—a kind of knowledge without which, in the case of contemporaries at least, one sometimes wonders (after Plato)[1] if it is possible to have any real insight into the spirit and tendencies of a man's thought. His thesis for the doctorate[2] was upon "Nietzsche's Idea of Culture", that which he wrote for his qualification as University teacher upon "The Philosophical Basis of the Biological Sciences", preceding his appointment as Lecturer in Philosophy first in Göttingen and then under Heidegger in Freiburg.

Readers will draw their own conclusions from his presentation of his subject in this book. As a student of the older German and particularly the Kantian philosophy, though comparatively a tiro in the study of

---

[1] "For the matter is not exponible in speech like other subjects. It is only after long fellowship in the business itself and in life together that so to say a light is kindled in one soul by the fire bursting forth from the other" (Epistle VII, p. 341 C).

[2] Published by Cohen, Bonn, in 1930. (Now obtainable from Schulte-Bulmke, Frankfurt a. M.)

what has been taking place in Germany in the interval, I have been struck by the evidence it seems to contain of a reaction in recent years in the direction of the great fundamentally humanitarian ideas of that earlier movement. If its publication should help to renew our sympathy with the deeper mind of his own great nation, which I for one believe to have remained faithful, in spite of violent cross-currents, to these ideas, it will be not less welcome from the side of contemporary politics than from that of contemporary philosophy.

J. H. MUIRHEAD

Rotherfield
April 11th, 1935

PREFACE

In May 1934 I delivered three lectures on Contemporary German Philosophy at Bedford College in the University of London and the substance of these lectures is presented in a revised and somewhat expanded form in this book.

In the course of the work its purpose will, I think, become sufficiently clear and therefore it need not be explained here. But I should like to draw attention to what in the lectures themselves remained in the background, though it is essential to an understanding of them—the unique position which in the last two centuries German philosophy has occupied in the intellectual life of the nation. For Philosophy, in its fullest sense, was in Germany regarded not as the business of private individuals who undertook either keen logical investigations, or metaphysical speculations which although penetrating were limited to their own experience, but as the work of those who felt themselves bound to give to the men of their age an interpretation of the world and an explanation of the principles of conduct, and who, for this double purpose, sought after truth.

This conception of philosophy is to be partly attributed to the lack of political unity, to the absence of a dominant class and to the fact that the character of the German people had not been formed by any one national ideal. For this kind of philosophy was able, by an insight into principles of an interpretation of the world and of the conduct of life, to offer to the individual an inner certainty and clearness which could compensate for the lack of universally accepted social conventions. But here it must be borne in mind that in the spiritual life of Germany philosophy was only a part of a greater whole; for philosophy which has developed from the background of Lutheran Protestantism, belonged, together with music, poetry and science, to what in contrast to the "civilisation" of the two great Western nations has been designated "Kultur". When Kant distinguished between philosophy in the sense of a school and philosophy in the universal sense and endeavoured to carry out his own work in obedience to this twofold demand, and when Hegel declared religion, art and knowledge to be the three manifestations of the absolute spirit, these conceptions of the two most powerful thinkers in German philosophy originated from the realisation of an autonomous Kultur that goes beyond the requirements of daily life without, however, extending to the Beyond in the Christian sense. One may even be reminded of the unique connection between art, poetry and philosophy in the Greece of the city states, when one observes the similar connection of great spiritual tendencies in the Kultur of Germany. Throughout this book, in which I endeavour to describe the development of German post-Hegelian philosophy, it will be well to bear in mind these conditions peculiar to the life of that country.

What, apart from this consideration, has induced me

briefly to indicate this background is the circumstance that the great change that has taken place in Germany makes it as yet impossible to foresee in what way the spiritual life of the nation will manifest itself in the future. Therefore on those German scholars who are now making their homes in foreign countries, yet who feel themselves bound in their very existence to the deepest impulses and the sublimest endeavours of German spiritual life, has fallen the burden of a not inconsiderable responsibility. They must try to render more accessible to other peoples what German men of genius have achieved in the course of the centuries. They have, so to speak, to ask the world whether what has been accomplished in Germany, but has hitherto exercised little influence outside that country, does not contain something of value to the other great nations. Whether and to what extent this is so is, of course, a matter for the other great nations, not for these men to decide. However, great as is the divergency between this task and the limited subject of this essay, I wish to state that this work has been undertaken with the realisation of this task, and that, when at the end I discuss the uncertainty of the fate of philosophy in the future and point in conclusion to the alternative between a philosophy that is only one of schools and a philosophy that is also universal, I am not, I believe, expressing a merely private opinion, but am trying to give words to the one question which German philosophy since Kant and Contemporary German Philosophy put to the men of our age.

*   *   *

PREFACE

With regard to the actual contents of the book, I wish to emphasise the point that this Introduction to Contemporary German Philosophy does not claim to offer a complete survey, treating proportionately the achievements of the different philosophical movements since Hegel. Such a complete survey would for instance have had to include a detailed study of so original a thinker as Husserl's master Brentano and an account of the views and influence of L. Nelson, the founder of the Neo-Friesian school; and it would also have had to describe more fully the work of recent and contemporary investigators such as Simmel, Scheler, N. Hartmann and Cassirer. Moreover, when discussing within the limits of the present study the work of Husserl, Dilthey and Weber; Nietzsche and Kierkegaard; Jaspers and Heidegger, I can do no more than direct attention to some not unimportant problems with which they have dealt; and it should be borne in mind that from the brief accounts here given it is not possible to form a critical estimate of the whole work of these men.

After the lectures had been delivered, some smaller parts were added; this has resulted in a certain lack of proportion for which I have to apologise. Moreover, the account of Max Weber seems to me particularly in need of explanation. It was written nearly a year after the lectures; and although my intention was to indicate Weber's place in the development of Contemporary German Philosophy, I had, nevertheless, his philosophical personality and his conception of "Wertfreiheit" even more before my mind, and consequently I fear that the detailed form and the contents of this account may have somewhat disturbed the balance of the first chapter. But what in spite of this defect has prevented me from reducing this part to a length more proportionate to the descriptions of the works of Husserl and Dilthey, was the impression that these have been dealt with rather too briefly, and the hope that by the somewhat fuller explanation of the "Wertfreiheit" the significance of Dilthey's understanding of the tension between Weltanschauung and Science and of Husserl's phenomenological method (problems to which I wish later to do more justice) could be made at least a little clearer. Furthermore, contrary to my usual custom in this book, I have discussed Weber's political and scientific endeavours at considerable length. This seemed to me permissible, since Weber's philosophical attitude was even more clearly manifested in his actions and specialised research than in his actual philosophical formulations. If there is truth in Nietzsche's conviction that genuine philosophy originates from love of wisdom, and that the individual will first prove this in his attitude towards the reality around him, before he ventures to formulate his philosophical conceptions, Weber was a philosopher in this concrete sense; and it would appear to be inappropriate to describe in isolation his abstract principle of "Wertfreiheit" without having previously indicated the actual life of which it is the philosophical consummation.

*   *   *

PREFACE

I have to thank Professor L. Susan Stebbing, who was the Chairman of my lectures and to whose interest and encouragement the publication of this book is primarily due. Several friends have assisted in preparing the final text for the press, and I wish especially to acknowledge the help of Mr H. W. B. Skinner, lecturer in the University of Bristol, and Mrs Skinner, and also of Miss K. L. Wood-Legh, Ph.D., of Cambridge. Further, I am much indebted to Professor J. H. Muirhead, the author of the Foreword, who in reading the manuscript has made helpful suggestions and whose advice in practical matters has been of great value. I wish also to thank my wife for constant help in all stages of the progress of this book. Finally, I wish to thank the University of London for the invitation to deliver the original course of lectures and the Faculty of Moral Science of Cambridge University and the Academic Assistance Council for financial assistance without which this book could not have been written. And in remembering with gratitude all the persons and institutions to whom this book is in any way indebted, I wish to express a still deeper gratitude to the two spiritual powers to which, in the fullest sense, this little work belongs—German Philosophy and English Hospitality.

WERNER BROCK

Cambridge
April 11th, 1935

CHAPTER I

THE BEGINNINGS OF
CONTEMPORARY GERMAN
PHILOSOPHY

In this Introduction to Contemporary German Philosophy I do not wish to survey all the trends of thought, which in Germany to-day are regarded as philosophical; nor shall I discuss here every recent philosophical work of note. I propose rather to restrict this account to what I believe presents the central problem of German philosophy during the last century and especially the last decades: What, in this age of science, is the task of philosophy, if any task still remains for it beyond the preservation and development of logic and the study of its own history?

This problem has been forced upon us by two intellectual events: first, by what is usually designated as the breakdown of Hegel's philosophy, which was due to a rejection of idealistic speculation in general; and secondly, by the growth in the nineteenth century of the separate sciences not merely of mathematics, physics and chemistry, but also of biology, sociology, psychology, history, and the humanistic sciences (Geisteswissenschaften).[1] Because scientific research

[1] Throughout this book, the term "Science" will be used not only for the Natural Sciences, but also for all other kinds of scientific study, including the Humanistic Sciences (Geisteswissenschaften).

was concerned equally with nature and with human life and was striving to explore the reality of all that exists, philosophy met with a serious crisis. For a fundamental issue arose: must philosophy be merged in science or has it nevertheless a task of its own? And if there should be such a task, of what significance, then, is the autonomous state of science and the reality investigated by the sciences?

German philosophy during the last century, in contrast to that which belongs to the period before Hegel and Schopenhauer, was confronted with this disquieting situation, which still forms the background of all contemporary philosophical endeavours. The problematic relation between Philosophy and Science, decisive for the character of German philosophy to-day, is comparable to the relation between Philosophy and Religion in the Middle Ages. My purpose here is to draw attention to those thinkers who in the new situation achieved the few important advances hitherto made towards the elucidation of the essence and the task of philosophy.

I

German Humanism and the development of the separate sciences as the background for Contemporary German Philosophy

For a comprehension of Contemporary German Philosophy, it is indispensable first to consider those two powerful movements which formed the intellectual setting for modern German thought. These movements are: (1) the philosophy of German Humanism (1775 to 1830), and (2) the development of the separate sciences since the third and fourth decades of the nineteenth century.

The significance of the philosophy of Fichte, Schelling, Hegel and Schleiermacher, as well as that of Kant, cannot be considered apart from other forms of German intellectual life in the second half of the eighteenth and the first decades of the nineteenth century, and from the remarkable fact that only in this period, and for the first time since the sixteenth century, there appeared in Germany a wide public with cultural interests. In the period from about 1775 to 1830, thought and poetry were intimately related, both being inspired by a humanism which was actually realised in the lives of the noblest men of the time. Lessing and Kant were those who, by their personal sincerity and intellectual force, led the movement of Enlightenment to its culmination: Lessing, who preferred the ceaseless search after truth to the mere acceptance even of complete truth and who set forth an ideal of tolerance, in which men of different creeds recognised their common brotherhood; Kant with his realisation of the limits of human understanding and with his reverence for freedom, followed in an unconditional devotion to the dictates of duty. After Hamann and Herder, who had speculated on the profound and intellectually inaccessible forces in nations, languages, art and religion, Goethe by his life and still more by his work gave expression to his faith that "all human deficiency can be atoned for by pure humanity", by the aspiring

3   1-2

efforts of the individual. To this faith men like Schiller and Wilhelm v. Humboldt adhered. Goethe's trusting acceptance of life and his attempt to find in all phenomena their deepest import dominated his poetry as well as his theory of colour and morphology. It was this specific approach to life and the world for which Fichte, Schelling and Schleiermacher tried to give philosophical justification; and this faith in humanity, lending to the Germans of those decades a nobility, a dignity and an enthusiasm hitherto rare, found its final intellectual expression in Hegel's philosophy, which aimed at penetrating all being and comprehending it in its true import, conceiving it as taken up and reconciled in the sphere of absolute spirit, beyond all human life, individual guilt and social injustice.

Other impulses moved these enquirers who, although they were originally inspired by the Romantic Movement or had started from Schelling's "Philosophy of Nature" or Hegel's "Philosophy of Mind", were left unsatisfied either by the prevailing indulgence in vague imaginings or by speculation in general; and who aimed instead at exploring reality in its separate manifestations.

Here, only very little can be said about the evolution of the inorganic sciences, which more than all the other branches of knowledge have developed internationally. The most important features, however, must be briefly mentioned: first of all the significance of the expansion of physics, beyond the limits of mechanics in Newton's sense, to include new branches, especially electricity; and also of the rise of chemistry. This development led in particular to a wealth of technical discoveries and,

4

in the intellectual sphere, to the quantum theory and the theory of relativity, which placed the problems of the atom and of the physical character of space-time as well as that of the perceptibility of physical objects on an entirely new basis.

In spite of the intellectual significance of these two theories, and although it cannot be doubted that the scientific exploration of inorganic nature, and its practical mastery by technical achievements must be an important subject for philosophical thought, it should not be supposed that physics in the nineteenth century had as a standard for philosophy the same significance that mathematics and physics in the seventeenth and eighteenth centuries had for Descartes, Leibniz or Kant. The trend of German philosophy in the last century, and indeed since Kant, cannot be properly understood, unless it is realised that within the domain of science mathematics and physics are no longer supreme, and that many other sciences, such as biology, sociology, psychology and history, are more important than mathematics and physics for the philosophy of recent times, and will probably remain so in the future. I cannot enter here into the reasons and significance of this change, and only wish to emphasise in this connection that among all the thinkers treated in these chapters, Husserl is the only one who started from the consideration of philosophical problems of mathematics.

It is therefore necessary to consider carefully the development of biology, which, after the preparatory morphological, physiological, embryological and systematic researches from the sixteenth to the eighteenth

century, came into its own only with Cuvier, Geoffroy St-Hilaire and Darwin. Among the German
scientists of the time after Goethe and Schelling the
embryologist Karl Ernst v. Baer and the anatomist and
physiologist Johann Müller must be mentioned as the
first important empiricists. The widespread influence
of Darwin in Germany, due to Haeckel, but also to such
eminent scientists as the embryologist Weismann and
the botanist Julius Sachs, is well known. What was
important in Darwin's work for our world-view was
that the relationship of man to the rest of living beings,
and even his origin from them, was recognised; and
that the actual importance of the dark emergence
of existence exemplified in the struggle and in the
destruction of the many was set forth. Of more
consequence to us, therefore, than the one-sided and
contestable Darwinian theory, was the consideration
without illusions of the origin of species and of man
as phenomena of this earthly existence, a conception
entirely opposed to the idealistic interpretation of man
in the age of Goethe. Later, Freud's exploration of
unconscious psychic life had a similar effect, though
progress in this field had previously been made by psychologists like Carus and Eduard v. Hartmann, and in
an entirely different way by Nietzsche. To sum up,
the course of development of the new sciences in the
nineteenth century was in one respect characterised by
the new significance acquired by biological studies and
by the change from the psychology of the conscious
(after the manner of Descartes, Locke, Hume, Leibniz,
or Herbart) to the psychology of the unconscious.

On the other hand, the development of historical and humanistic sciences (Geschichts- und Geisteswissenschaften) since the later part of the eighteenth century is of very great importance. In Germany during this period there grew up a large group of sciences: political history, economics, law and political science, mythology and comparative religion, as well as the study of art, poetry, music and literature, considered as products of various ages and nations. In these sciences—owing to Herder's intuitive perception of the independent value of every nation and age, to Friedrich and August Wilhelm Schlegel's realisation of the variety of different kinds of language and literature and their methodical principle of "inner form", to Schleiermacher's hermeneutic and to Friedrich August Wolf's and v. Humboldt's methods of philology—a new type of research was created, different in character from, but equal in the strictness of its critical methods to that of the natural sciences of two centuries earlier. The great common achievement of these sciences consisted in basing the investigation of the spiritual and intellectual life on historical and social facts. In Niebuhr's Roman history, Savigny's investigations of law and its history, Jacob Grimm's conceptions of the development of the German spirit in language, law and religion, in Boeckh's and Otfried Müller's classical philology, this one great tendency found expression. And after Hegel had supplemented these efforts by the principle of a universal history, in Ranke's political history, Karl Marx's economic analysis, and Burckhardt's history of culture was created a new attitude

7

towards the spiritual and intellectual life, starting from which the richness and individuality of reality, experienced by men and pursued in their works, were investigated, and the determining forces in the social and political life of the past, the rise and fall of whole nations, the dependence of great men on social powers and historical currents, and the inter-relation between State, Religion and Culture became apparent.

No better characterisation of scientific research during the nineteenth century, in contrast to German idealism as a whole, can be found than the dictum of the great economist and sociologist, Max Weber: "A disenchantment of the world is taking place." A desire was felt to see all reality, past and present, clearly and without illusions; the close relationship of man to animal, the organised struggle for power in society and political states and even spiritual life, still in contact with the dark and the all-too-human by which it is surrounded and from which it is itself seldom quite free. And while German Humanism sought in everything, even in nature, the significant and the sublime, the nineteenth century doubted everything from the very beginning, examining thoroughly and accepting only what proved to be indubitable. The real contiguity between the world and human life, the manifold dependencies of man on external and internal causes in nature, society and history, were set forth as dispassionately and precisely as possible. And although the prevailing tendency was towards materialism, yet eminent scholars like Jacob Burckhardt investigated the facts of life with a disinterested love of truth and

8

an equanimity which enabled them to acknowledge more clearly than ever before reality, even in its manifold senseless and painful aspects. Such general tendencies of thought formed the background for the extraordinary richness of knowledge in the separate sciences.

2

Two new philosophical movements since Hegel: attempts towards a philosophical synthesis of scientific results; and epistemological enquiries

In the midst of such activity, after the decline of German Humanism and contemporaneously with the newly emerging separate sciences and the belated fame of Schopenhauer's work, which at that time seemed to earnest and resigned thinkers to offer an expression of profound truth, began those endeavours from which our present-day philosophy has developed. The vital question, then as now, was, as has been said above, what, in the era of such sciences, is the real task of philosophy?

The first answer given to this question was: philosophy has, in metaphysics, to bring about a synthesis of scientific results. Its aim must be, as Wundt says, "the construction of a logically consistent world-view which shall bring all special knowledge into one general system of thought". Here Wundt distinguishes between "that which is given in experience", that is, from which we have to start, and the "ultimate causes, not given in experience", and he requires from meta-

9

physics as its chief task that such a synthesis be accomplished by proceeding inductively from what is given in experience to the ultimate causes.

It was in this way that the three most important scientific metaphysicians of the second half of the nineteenth century, Fechner, Lotze and Eduard v. Hartmann, conceived their philosophical task. From a scientific basis they outlined metaphysics in different ways: Fechner in a synthesis of Romantic philosophy of Nature and experimental research, Lotze in a reconciliation of mechanical investigation and an idealistic world-view, Eduard v. Hartmann in a combination of physiological and psychological results with the speculation of Schelling, Schopenhauer and Hegel. But they thereby gave satisfaction neither to science nor to philosophy.

Science was not satisfied, for the following reasons. In seeking to bring together scientific results to form one whole, these scholars did not consider whether it was at all possible to combine scientific results in a logically consistent whole, that is, whether there might not be such deep contradictions within all cognisable reality that the system of one uniform whole produced an illusion rather than a unification and summary of truth. Nor did they respect the objectivity of scientific investigation, with its claim to universal validity, inasmuch as they proceeded to ultimate causes that went beyond experience and were therefore no longer demonstrable. Moreover, none of these synthesising thinkers was able to present a description of reality in so direct, so deep and so convincing a way, as is done by the specialised researcher, at home in his particular branch of knowledge. For it is characteristic of genuine research, though it be concerned only with one aspect of reality, to penetrate to, and to make known, truth, in a way which is impossible to those who merely utilise the results obtained by others.[1]

But at the same time these men failed to fulfil the demand of philosophy, since they, inspired by forceful fragments of the idealistic metaphysics of the past which chanced to influence them, drew from certain scientific results an arbitrary interpretation of the world, which had merely subjective value. Instead of considering the essence of science and the specific character of philosophy, or of penetrating into the meaning of the collapse of idealistic speculation, which would have enabled them through increased clearness to attempt a new manner of philosophising, they pursued a course which we can now see to have been erroneous, that of eclecticism with regard to both philosophy and science.

Yet in spite of the failure of this first movement of contemporary philosophy to satisfy critical claims, its exponents are of importance because, in an age of great scientific productivity and of almost complete philosophical sterility, they have the credit of following the sincere desire to proceed beyond science to a world-view, even though their philosophical power and insight into principles were far inferior to those of a Fichte, a Schelling, a Hegel or a Schleiermacher.

[1] This criticism, of course, refers only to the philosophical work of these scholars, not to their genuinely scientific work.

A second group of philosophers gave to the fundamental question of the task of philosophy an entirely different answer: they did not aim at presenting a philosophical world-view nor did they seek to synthesise scientific results. But, inspired by the question: how is scientific knowledge at all possible? they enquired into the presuppositions, principles and methods which are not investigated by the sciences themselves. Through such researches concerning the problems and critique of knowledge, philosophy gained for itself a definite sphere of enquiry which belonged to no other science. This meant in fact the development of a science of scientific thinking and research; while other philosophical tasks, such as those of Ethics and Aesthetics, did not in the same way receive adequate treatment, but were carried out—either in the traditional metaphysical way or from an epistemological point of view, or by the methods employed in the separate sciences—according to the personal convictions of the individual researchers. It was through the discussion of these epistemological problems that German philosophy in the last third of the past century assumed its "academic" character. The philosophers themselves took up a scientific attitude; and though they renounced essential, and probably even the main, tasks of philosophy, the movement has, in spite of its limitations, been surprisingly productive, and has rendered possible all future developments.

The thinker who was most representative of this movement was Ernst Cohen, the founder of the Marburg neo-Kantian school; following Kant's *Critique of*

Pure Reason, he concentrated on these problems of the possibility of knowledge and of the presuppositions and principles of scientific research. And, granted that the researches of the many schools to which this movement gave rise, did not, and probably indeed could not, elucidate the essence of scientific knowledge itself, in spite of the various positivist, pragmatist, fictionist or intellectualist theories of knowledge; much that is valid was discovered about the specific character of the separate sciences and about the various spheres of reality to which they are related.

Thus, for instance, the particularity of the psychic in contrast to the physical was investigated by such enquirers as Dilthey, Jaspers and Klages in a way entirely different from the traditional constructive psychology built after the model of the natural sciences.[1] The difference between the historical and natural sciences was formulated by Windelband and Rickert, and more deeply thought out and understood by

[1] When here Dilthey, Weber, Jaspers and others are mentioned with regard to their achievements in the theory of knowledge of the separate sciences, this does not contradict the fact that by the influence of these men the exclusively epistemological tendency in contemporary philosophy has been overcome. On the contrary, it is characteristic of the development of contemporary German philosophy that precisely those scholars who were at home in their branches of science and were intent upon finding their principles came to be the men who recognised with especially clear insight the limitations of science and the deeper philosophical tasks. This results from the peculiar relation of philosophy to science during the last century, emphasised at the beginning.

Dilthey. The abstention from valuations in the economic and sociological sciences was postulated by Max Weber, and, conversely, the significance of valuations for the research that interprets spiritual and intellectual phenomena was brought out by Gundolf's investigations into the history of literature. The character of living being, in contrast to non-living being, was elaborated by Driesch; and it was this recognition of the peculiar character of one group of sciences, not his metaphysical speculations, which gave to Driesch's "Vitalism" its importance. The principle that all logical structures should be considered independently of psychological processes and of the explanation of their origins, was demonstrated by Husserl. I content myself with the mention of these few most important achievements concerning the theory of knowledge, and I wish further to emphasise only the fact that, when Nicolai Hartmann and Jaspers to-day distinguish four entirely different spheres of reality, those of matter, life, soul and mind, their insight is based on decades of investigation by academic philosophers, but that such researches, far from having come to an end, are still continuously in progress, pointing the way towards new and more fundamental discoveries.

Though these results were remarkable enough to establish the value of this movement, it has become especially important, because it included three scholars, who, through their efforts to provide a foundation for certain sciences, arrived at philosophical results of far-reaching consequence: Husserl, Dilthey and Weber.

3

Husserl

Husserl's significance for German philosophical development is primarily due to the fact that, proceeding from a philosophy of arithmetic, he established in his *Logische Untersuchungen* the autonomy of logic, especially as opposed to the hitherto dominant psychological logic, influenced by Mill. This he accomplished partly by a general explanation (the "Prolegomena to Pure Logic", volume I of the *Logische Untersuchungen*); but above all by his own productive research into the phenomenology of knowledge, constituting the second volume. Here, beginning with the problem of the meaning of linguistic expression, he discovered a new method, that of phenomenological analysis; the fundamental significance of which he later endeavoured to present in his *Ideen zu einer reinen Phänomenologie und phänomenologischen Philosophie*. To convey at least a slight impression of the peculiar character of this phenomenological method, I should like to begin with a distinction stressed by Husserl himself and common to all different phenomenological tendencies, the distinction between fact and essence.[1]

In daily life and in the empirical sciences, we derive our ordinary knowledge from the experience of facts. In such acts of experience, we perceive real things as individual, and we describe in them individual peculiarities. For example, this table in front of me is of this particular height and width, of just this shape, made of

[1] *Ideen zu einer reinen Phänomenologie und phänomenologischen Philosophie*, S. 7–32 (Abschnitt I, Kap. I).

this particular wood, of just this shade of brown, placed in this room, in such and such a manner, at this moment, and so on. All these details may be actually perceived and asserted about the writing table. But this is possible, because any single actual object such as a writing table possesses its peculiar character, that is, a group of essential predicables belonging to it, and because of this peculiar character we perceive properties such as height or width or shape belonging to the essence of an individual object. That is to say: we not only see in this table here special characteristics, that are peculiar to it, but we also perceive intuitively definite general and essential features (for instance, its being a physical body or a constructed instrument), which we meet with in this table, and which to us are actually represented and exemplified in this individual object. And such general and essential features, according to Husserl, are not only to be found intuitively in all individual phenomena that are experienced, but we have always at our disposal a variety of such more or less clearly intuited features both in memory and in imagination, in which we can produce spatial forms, melodies, social processes, and also acts of experience, of satisfaction and dissatisfaction, and so on. Moreover, in geometry, according to Husserl, we have a science in which one does not at all start from empirical facts, but from the intuition of certain ideal essentials such as a point, line, triangle. And it is the conviction of Husserl and the other phenomenologists, that philosophy is likewise concerned with the intuitive apprehension and exact description of such essentials. This means that its primary task is to make clear in intellectual intuition what extended things, psychic experiences, volitions, really are as phenomena, of what their structural properties consist, how the individual features are to be differentiated and conceptually described. All this must be done in order to represent the full conceptual content which belongs to the phenomena of an extended thing, a psychic experience, a volition. When Husserl, however, comprehends phenomenological philosophy as a science of essence (Wesenswissenschaft) like geometry or arithmetic, there is a fundamental difference, in that phenomenology is not, as the other special sciences, directed towards any one limited field of essentials, but has for its task the analysis and description of all the basic essences, which we constantly employ, in our ordinary language and in our scientific research, for the most part without having explicitly realised their full meaning. Such a general clarification of the meaning of phenomena on the basis of attentive intuition and carefully analysed conceptual description, as was begun by Husserl himself in the *Logische Untersuchungen*, was the first and principal demand which his Phenomenology brought forward; and which was carried out by his collaborators and disciples in the analysis of such very different phenomena as aesthetic enjoyment, ethical values, law, volition and the unconscious psychic.

But it should be observed that Husserl's own philosophical enquiries only begin with this distinction between fact and essence. While other phenomenologists, such as Pfänder, Geiger and Scheler, were content to employ Husserl's method for the analysis and description of various phenomena and problems, Husserl himself undertook the specific task of a phenomenological investigation of "pure consciousness" in its entire domain, including its "acts" and their "intended objects". This task, in which culminated the epistemological movement in the German philosophy of that time, Husserl tried to accomplish by a radical change in our natural attitude towards the real world, this change being called "the phenomenological ἐποχή". This means that we should abstain from attributing to any of our conscious experiences and judgments the character of reality. In this fundamental phenomenological attitude, we purposely overlook the reality of all that to which our consciousness is directed as well as the character of reality of consciousness itself, and assume that this will not change either the intended objects (facts and essences), or the acts of our consciousness. It is, therefore, only the character of reality which has to be "bracketed", or rather "suspended", an attempt analogous to that made by Descartes in his second "Meditation" to doubt everything. In this attitude, Husserl does not follow the sceptics in doubting it. On the contrary, the purpose of this attitude is only methodological; it aims at a clearer grasp and a more accurate description of pure consciousness with its "noetic-noematic structures".[1]

[1] The phenomenological ἐποχή is described in *Ideen*, Abschnitt II, S. 48 ff., the structural problems of pure consciousness in *Ideen*, Abschnitte III und IV, S. 141 ff.

In these two achievements, the elaboration of the phenomenological method, and the attempt at a radical analysis of pure consciousness with the help of this phenomenology, lies Husserl's philosophical importance. These two achievements, however, have not received equal attention. The peculiarity and significance of the phenomenological method was soon appreciated and has been very influential in contemporary German philosophy; whereas the second, and for Husserl himself the chief, aspect of his work, although it was esteemed by the older epistemological schools, especially by the Neo-Kantians of Marburg, exercised little influence on the other phenomenologists. Only Heidegger, later, followed this type of radical analysis, aiming, however, at a completely different task by substituting the analysis of human existence for the analysis of pure consciousness. Here, therefore, we may pass over the problems involved in Husserl's "analysis of pure consciousness" and examine only the methodological character of phenomenology in its significance for contemporary philosophy.

Phenomenology is quite distinct from syntheses of Weltanschauung, in the sense of Wundt, and from the positivist or intellectualist construction of systems, usual up to that time. It teaches us, instead, to concentrate on single phenomena in order to intuit their full conceptual meaning, and to analyse this meaning in its true complexity, not resting content with simple dogmatic solutions. The method of phenomenology is thus more akin to that of the separate sciences in its manner of intuiting, observing, analysing, distinguishing and describing, than to philosophical construction with ultimate standpoints and all-determining principles.

While Husserl in this way gave a method of analysis to contemporary philosophers, inspiring and training them for systematic research, there is, nevertheless, as can be seen clearly from the development of phenomenology in the last thirty years, a certain danger inherent in the exclusively methodological character of his work. Only a few investigators have by following this method discovered new structural connections and properties in philosophically relevant phenomena. To take examples from the older phenomenologists, I may mention Scheler's treatise on the "Ethics of Material Values", and Geiger's fragment on the "Unconscious Psychic". But, in course of time, numerous studies appeared in which this method was applied to less important and sometimes even to very limited phenomena, thus contributing to separate sciences rather than to philosophy. It is the peculiarity and the danger of the phenomenological method that the choice of the problems rests entirely with the individual investigator.

4

Dilthey

Dilthey grew up in the school of great historians, such as Boeckh, Jacob Grimm and Ranke, who gave him a scientific outlook on the life of nations and the political history of the world. To the lasting impressions derived from these studies, Dilthey, as he himself

DILTHEY

has said, owed the whole trend of his thought. His aim was to investigate the nature and conditions of historical consciousness, or, as he expressed it, borrowing the language, and, in one respect, carrying forward the work, of Kant, to give a "Critique of Historical Reason". The great fragments of which his work consists are devoted to this task, the profound significance of which has only gradually, during the last twenty years, begun to be perceived in Germany.

I pass over his researches into the history of intellectual life, in which he traced the growth of the modern "Lebens- und Weltanschauung" from the sixteenth to the nineteenth century,[1] and also his studies on the history of poetry and music,[2] and call attention only to his *Einleitung in die Geisteswissenschaften* (a term of which he established the use), published in 1883, and which like Husserl's *Logische Untersuchungen* has now become a classic.[3] In this Dilthey, more than a decade before the incomparably weaker characterisation of the historical sciences by Windelband and Rickert appeared, explained the interconnection of the various "Geisteswissenschaften" and their relation to life in society and history. The underlying intention of this work is to prepare the unitary foundation for all these sciences. The demand for such a foundation he supported by an analysis of European philosophy from its beginnings up to Hegel, in which he sought to show the inner reasons for the former

[1] *Gesammelte Werke*, Bd. II, III und IV.
[2] *Erlebnis und Dichtung* and *Von deutscher Dichtung und Musik*.
[3] *Gesammelte Werke*, Bd. I.

21

predominance, and for the inevitable decline of metaphysics.

Later, he himself made two attempts to lay the foundation which he thought necessary: first, in the 'eighties and 'nineties, he outlined in contrast to the usual psychology with its causal explanations, a descriptive, analytic and understanding psychology ("beschreibende, zergliedernde und verstehende Psychologie"), which, instead of trying by a kind of mental "chemistry" to construct all mental phenomena out of simple elements, aimed at analysing and describing the full realities of psychic life in a new way that would not mutilate them.[1] With this understanding, analytic and descriptive psychology, he prepared the method for a new and important type of psychology in Germany, though he did not succeed in his more general plan of laying a sure foundation for the "Geisteswissenschaften".

Late in life, between 1900 and 1910, Dilthey, who meanwhile had reached the conclusion, confirmed by Husserl's *Logische Untersuchungen*, that the investigation of the basis of the "Geisteswissenschaften" does not require the support of such a special type of psychology, made his second attempt. In this second attempt he sought, by developing a new "Hermeneutik", to explain the building up of our historical world for which experience (Erlebnis), expression (Ausdruck) and understanding (Verstehen) are the three determining factors, and for which the "Geisteswissen-

[1] "Ideen über eine beschreibende und zergliedernde Psychologie", *Gesammelte Werke*, Bd. v, S. 139–240.

schaften" must be of ever-increasing importance.¹ And
although this endeavour remained likewise incomplete,
Dilthey's work has a force and depth of reflection far
surpassing that of all his successors, such as Troeltsch,
and still points the way into the future.

However, just as Husserl in his *Logische Untersuchungen* discovered more than the independence of
logic from psychology, so Dilthey's philosophical
importance is not limited to his attempts at discovering
the foundations of the "Geisteswissenschaften".
"Critique of Historical Reason" means more than this.
It is not only concerned with a group of sciences, but
it arises out of the self-knowledge of philosophy that
all philosophising, and in truth all branches of learning,
are bound up with historical human life, originating
from it and reacting upon it.

In order to understand clearly the essence of philosophy, the reason for the collapse of metaphysics and
the future task of philosophy, Dilthey examined critically the history of philosophy. For, as he says: "The
question, what is philosophy, cannot be answered according to the taste of the individual, since its function
can only be empirically deduced from history."²

Its function—by this is meant its real significance
for the spiritual life of the individual and of society.
Starting from this conception, Dilthey recognised that
no doubt one essential aim of philosophy, especially

¹ "Der Aufbau der geschichtlichen Welt in den Geistes-
wissenschaften", *Gesammelte Werke*, Bd. VII, S. 79–188, and
"Erleben, Ausdruck und Verstehen", *Gesammelte Werke*, Bd. VII,
S. 191–251.   ² Dilthey, *Gesammelte Werke*, Bd. VIII, S. 189.

since Socrates and Plato, was to demonstrate the order of the world in a universally acceptable scientific manner, that is, in a way consistent with objective thought and exact examination. Thus metaphysics, as developed in Greece after the model of geometrical thinking, is that form of philosophy which treats the order of the world scientifically, as if it were entirely objective, independent of the life of man. But, according to Dilthey, what at all times has given a deeper impulse to philosophy is the desire originating from the experiences of life to attain a unitary attitude towards the perplexing riddle of life and the world.

The insolubility of this riddle has led to the divergency of views on life and the world, expressed in the various religions and in another way in every great art. Philosophical systems, likewise, express such Weltanschauungen—to which circumstance is largely due the power which philosophy exerts over mankind—but with the difference that philosophy, at least until Hegel, has assumed the possibility of finding a universally acceptable logical proof for such Weltanschauungen. Dilthey, however, recognised that a Weltanschauung can no longer be proved scientifically, and that it was this separation of Weltanschauung from scientific proof which had brought about the crisis of philosophy after Hegel.[1]

---

[1] The phenomenon of Weltanschauung, as elaborated by Dilthey—it was he who also settled the meaning of this term—is, of course, not to be identified with the conceptions of Weltanschauung which occur in the widespread and often misunderstood popularisation of Dilthey's thought.

Investigations which by such reflection on history aimed at penetrating into the essence of philosophy Dilthey termed "Philosophy of Philosophy". During fifty years of his life he pursued these studies, because he recognised "that concerning the concept of philosophy far less had hitherto been really ascertained, not merely proclaimed in moments of enthusiasm, than concerning that of religion".[1] This investigation was dominated by the antinomy between the claim of every philosophical Weltanschauung to universal validity, and the historical consciousness of the variety of such Weltanschauungen. Dilthey tried to elucidate this antinomy by reflecting on the full reality of life, out of which philosophical concepts originate. "The fundamental thought of my philosophy", he says, "is that hitherto the whole of unmutilated experience has never been made the basis of philosophy."[2] The necessity of advancing beyond Kant's intellectual and logical self-knowledge to the historical self-knowledge of philosophy, beyond a "Critique of Pure Reason" to a "Critique of Historical Reason" was the essential teaching of Dilthey's philosophy.[3]

And although he has carried through such a "historical reflection", such a "philosophy of philosophy"

[1] From his diary of 1859, published in *Der junge Dilthey*, S. 79.
[2] *Gesammelte Werke*, Bd. VIII, S. 175.
[3] Dilthey's "Philosophy of Philosophy", including his analysis of Weltanschauung and scientific proof, is given in "Das Wesen der Philosophie" (*Gesammelte Werke*, Bd. V, S. 339–416) and in "Weltanschauungslehre; Abhandlungen zur Philosophie der Philosophie" (*Gesammelte Schriften*, Bd. VIII).

only in imperfect fragments without reaching a conclusion, he has contributed more than any other academic philosopher to the elucidation of the peculiar situation of philosophy since Hegel. He likewise endeavoured to make men again aware of the great tasks of philosophy extending beyond the limits of mere science, and of the great difficulties which these tasks present when universally valid objective argumentation is demanded, and now that the divergence of Weltanschauung and Science is recognised.

5
Weber

Besides Husserl and Dilthey, a third thinker should be mentioned: the sociologist Max Weber. There is, no doubt, a distinction between him and the other two in that he remained throughout his life a scientist, and although exerting an inspiring influence on Jaspers, he did not found a philosophical school. Nevertheless, he seems to have resembled Dilthey and Husserl in the course of his intellectual development. First, in studies of Law, Economics and Sociology, he tried to attain a thorough knowledge of each of a group of separate sciences, in the same way as Dilthey studied the history of the Humanistic Sciences and Husserl studied Mathematics and Logic. Like these two, he then endeavoured to clarify the epistemological premises and the methodological principles of his group of sciences in order to lay an adequate philosophical foundation for them. Finally, he advanced beyond this to a still more fundamental conception which is especially significant for the general relation between science and philosophy: his conception of "Wertfreiheit" (necessity of abstaining from valuations) in Science. This conception is comparable in importance to Husserl's discovery of the phenomenological method and to Dilthey's insight into the tension between Weltanschauung and Science.

Weber distinguished himself from all the other eminent thinkers of the last decades by the character of his work in that he was both a scientist and a politician. And this circumstance adds weight to his doctrine of the "Wertfreiheit" of science. For the more intensely he pursued, in politics, the realisation of certain values, the more clearly he realised that—if the social sciences were ever to rise to the rank of objective sciences which could furnish men in industry and politics with a thorough and reliable knowledge, such as that which physics supplies to the engineer—they must be kept free from the manifold and divergent valuations which until now had continuously hindered a methodical statement of the facts and the objective analysis of the determining factors of social life. Before turning to an analysis of what is meant by Weber's conception of "Wertfreiheit" beyond its immediately evident significance for the social sciences, his political and scientific work, which forms the background for this philosophically important conception, may be briefly reviewed.

His whole political action was based upon his concern for the future of Germany as one of the great

European powers and upon his belief in the dignity of the independent individual. His deep-rooted fear, felt since the 'nineties, for the future of his country was due to the observation that in German political life there was a serious lack of trained and responsible leaders, and that Germany was forced to choose her leading statesmen chiefly from a bureaucracy which, though conscientious and submissive to discipline, was entirely unprepared for political initiative and independent action. Moreover, he was from the beginning aware of the fact that no class, neither the declining Junker-class, nor the bourgeoisie which was then at the height of its power, nor the rising working-class, was sufficiently mature to assume the leadership of the nation. Accordingly he regarded the political education of his countrymen in national and social matters as a duty incumbent upon himself; this task he took up in the 'nineties and, after the interruption caused by years of illness, he continued it during the War and the revolution. Furthermore, throughout the War, he tried to assist the German government in critical situations by offering prudent advice, for example by a paper warning against the policy of unrestricted submarine warfare and anticipating the probability and the consequences of the entry of the United States into the War. But such attempts to avert errors of policy which were decisive of Germany's fate continually failed.[1]

As an investigator of social problems Weber was at once historian, theorist and methodologist. Just as in

[1] "Politische Schriften." The paper on submarine warfare, S. 64–72.

politics he was equally remarkable for breadth of vision and for a power of estimating accurately all the factors of a situation, in science he was constantly concerned with fundamental problems, without feeling the investigation of the minutest detail to be beneath his attention.

As a social historian he was especially occupied with the origin of Western Capitalism and its significance in human development. These problems gave rise to his well-known study of the connection between protestant faith and capitalist methods of business and to his investigations into the effects of religion upon the social life of the Chinese, the Indians and the ancient Jews. In the former, a positive critique of the Marxian interpretation of history, he tried to analyse the influence exerted on economic life by a conception purely spiritual in origin, the Lutheran idea of "calling" and the Calvinistic idea of "justification by merit"; in the latter, he sought through an examination of other civilisations to explain by contrast what the rationalistic capitalism of the West really signified and what other possibilities of the religious influence on the formation of society it had excluded.[1] Throughout this work he was always aware that he was directing attention to only one hitherto neglected factor in the origin of Capitalism, and that nothing could be more detrimental to a true historical understanding than a dogmatic interpretation based on the recognition of only one factor, be it material or spiritual. For, according to Weber, it is precisely the task of history, by an analysis

[1] *Gesammelte Aufsätze zur Religionssoziologie.*

of the, theoretically infinite, number of causal connections to convey a more and more adequate realisation
of how and why any given event could have taken
place.[1] Such an inner freedom from dogma and open-
mindedness towards the ascertainable causal connections in social history and social science was the
underlying principle in all Weber's scientific work,
which included monographs dealing with the most
varied spheres of economic life in the most widely
different periods, such as the history of Roman agrarian
problems, the decline of the ancient world, the medieval
trading companies, the agricultural labourers east of
the Elbe, the stock-exchange, or the psychophysics of
industrial work.

While Weber as a universal historian of social and
economic life was carrying out his detailed and concrete
investigations, as a critical thinker he tried at the same
time to make clear the terms in which social problems
must be described and analysed. Thus, in the first part
of his chief theoretical work *Wirtschaft und Gesellschaft*, which is a model of logical thought, an exposition of the fundamental sociological definitions is
given. This teaching is entirely derived from his
historical researches. It was reached by induction
during the development of his insight into the manifold
causal connections in society and history, and was
definitely established only towards the end of his life.

But Weber did not restrict himself to the logical

[1] "Objektive Möglichkeit und adäquate Verursachung in der
historischen Kausalbetrachtung" in *Gesammelte Aufsätze zur
Wissenschaftslehre*, S. 266 ff.

explanation of the terms which he employed. He was equally careful to define and analyse the methods which he used and which he believed must be used, if the social sciences were to be treated objectively. In accordance with this purpose of methodological elucidation he examined and criticised the methods of previous and contemporary economists and historians. Furthermore, he himself described some methodological principles, among which his concept of the construction of "ideal types" (Idealtypen) as one means for the classification and the comprehension of actual, that is individual, historical and social connections,[1] and his explanations of "objective possibility" (objektive Möglichkeit) and "adequate comprehension of causation" (adäquate Verursachung) in the analysis of causal connections in history are especially noteworthy. This requirement of methodological reflection has also given rise to Weber's doctrine of the "Wertfreiheit" of Science. And this doctrine had, beyond its purely methodological significance, a philosophical bearing; for not only does it make clear the relation between social knowledge and political action, but it also answers the broader question of the importance of scientific knowledge in determining thought and conduct in practical affairs.[2]

[1] *Gesammelte Aufsätze zur Wissenschaftslehre*, S. 190–205.

[2] The subject of "Wertfreiheit" of science is discussed in several passages of Weber's work; its significance for the economic and sociological sciences is explained in "Der Sinn der 'Wertfreiheit' der soziologischen und ökonomischen Wissenschaften" (*Gesammelte Aufsätze zur Wissenschaftslehre*, S. 451

In his more general reflections, Weber started from two facts which to him seemed incontrovertible: the specialised character and the progressive tendency of science. He was fully conscious that science was and would continue to be a task for specialists and not a part of the speculations of philosophers on the meaning of the world. He realised also that true scientific achievement, although of course the unaccountable element of inventiveness must always play an important part, can only be attained as a result of strict specialisation. But any achievement in specialised science brings with it the prospect that later scientists will advance farther than the original discoverer. "Every scientific achievement raises new problems and requires to be surpassed and to become obsolete."[1] Science, in contrast for instance to art, is, in theory, bound to progress, and such progress, again theoretically, continues indefinitely. On these two premises depends the problem of the significance of science, the question namely: Has science, which is governed by this strange law, that the individual researcher must specialise as far as possible in order to be fitted for discovery and yet that neither he nor presumably any of his successors will reach the ultimate end even of his specialised knowledge, any significance in itself and, if so, what is this

bis 502) and its philosophical bearing in "Wissenschaft als Beruf". The account here given is based mainly on the relevant passages in "Wissenschaft als Beruf", but also on "Der Sinn der 'Wertfreiheit' der soziologischen und ökonomischen Wissenschaften" and on "Politik als Beruf".

[1] "Wissenschaft als Beruf", S. 14.

significance? (It may be well to mention here that the problem of the significance of science as based on the two facts of its specialisation and progressive character did not originate with Weber, but was first enunciated by Nietzsche, from whom Weber apparently derived it.)

In the characteristic answer which Weber gives to this question he distinguishes between the practical-technical significance of science and the significance which beyond this limit it has in itself.

The practical-technical significance of science he finds in the process of intellectual development achieved in the course of many centuries by the Occident, resulting in the "disenchantment of the world", that is, in the belief supported by manifold detailed knowledge that, in theory, there are no mysterious and inscrutable powers, and that, in theory, all things could be mastered by rationalising. From this point of view, science and the practical-technical results of science constitute the antithesis to the magic of savages. When, among the types of human conduct, besides those determined by custom and those resulting from the emotions and passions of the moment, both of which are leading motives everywhere and at all times, Weber distinguishes a "zweckrationales Handeln", he intends to describe conduct based on the assumptions that the outer world and other people will "behave" in certain calculable ways, and on the use of these "assumptions" for the attainment of any given purpose.[1] Such "zweckrationales Handeln", of course, has been to

[1] *Wirtschaft und Gesellschaft*, S. 12–13.

some extent practised in virtually all civilisations, but has been realised in principle, and in the deeper sense consistently, only in Western civilisation, and this chiefly owing to science. Herein, then, lies its practical-technical significance.[1]

When Weber enquires further concerning the real significance of science in itself, he sees clearly, as Nietzsche did before him, that the answer which has to be given to this problem to-day must be entirely different from those which it has received in the past. Formerly science was regarded as the way to true Being, or true Art, or true Nature, or the true God, or true Happiness. None of these definitions can now be accepted.

But still another interpretation of the meaning of science which was attempted in Weber's own time seemed to him illusory: namely the conviction that science could offer the means of understanding objectively the scale of values in human existence, and thus could decide for man what values he should aim at in his life, and what attitude he should adopt in difficult and perplexing situations. In other words, Weber declared, the purpose of science is not to show the "way to true Values".

The reason for this negative definition with regard to the purpose of science does not in Weber's case spring

[1] "Wissenschaft als Beruf", S. 15–16; see also *Gesammelte Aufsätze zur Religionssoziologie*, Bd. I, S. 1–16. In an interesting article, "Die rationalen und soziologischen Grundlagen der Musik" (München, 1921), he discusses the influence of rationality on the development of music in the West.

from the assumption that, beyond the attainment of individual practical-technical ends, there is no realisation of values in human existence. From his knowledge of history and from his own wide experience, Weber understood the realities of human existence too well to deny that men may act in conformity with ideals and principles to which they feel themselves entirely bound, and which they pursue for their own sake without regard to outward consequences. He would apply the term "wertrational" (in contrast to "zweckrational") to those persons whose life is dominated by such values as beauty, goodness, honour, religious faith or absolute devotion to duty.[1] What Weber doubted, therefore, is not the fact that values are pursued in human life, but only the power of science to make evident a single scale of values as objectively acceptable. The reason for the inability of science to do this is in Weber's opinion that the different values cannot be arranged harmoniously in one universally binding scale, but that on the contrary a "struggle between values" is in theory beyond decision and in reality is endless.[2]

The apostles of the German Humanism of about 1800 believed in a harmony of the good, the beautiful, the true and the holy. Weber doubted the possibility of such a harmony. He points to the fifty-third chapter of Isaiah and to the twenty-first Psalm, where there is

[1] *Wirtschaft und Gesellschaft*, S. 12–13.

[2] In "Wissenschaft als Beruf", S. 26 ff., and even more fully in "Der Sinn der 'Wertfreiheit' etc." (*Gesammelte Aufsätze zur Wissenschaftslehre*), especially S. 469 f.

evidence that a thing can be holy not merely although, but actually because and in so far as it is not beautiful; he recalls the thoughts of Baudelaire and Nietzsche with regard to a similar relationship between the good and the beautiful; and he draws attention to the every-day knowledge that a thing can be true, although at the same time it is neither beautiful nor holy nor good.

Similarly Weber disputes the possibility of the Church's succeeding in its attempt to establish a universally valid scale of values. Thus he was con-vinced that the "command" of the Sermon on the Mount: "Resist not evil!" a command which Jesus, the apostles, Francis of Assisi and certain other saints con-sistently obeyed, was irreconcilably opposed to the other command originating from the inner dignity of the free individual: "Resist evil; for otherwise thou shalt be an accomplice in its increase!" And he who is not a "saint" and is not ready to follow the commands of the Sermon on the Mount unconditionally and with-out regard to all the possible evil consequences—a politician for instance, whatever may be his ultimate values—must obey the human command, even when, as Weber once said, by so doing he offends the Christian God.

That this "struggle between values", from which Weber starts, has not until recently been truly appre-hended (only Nietzsche, who here also anticipates Weber, by his thought on the "revaluation of all values" circled around this intellectual fact, without, however, gaining a logically and philosophically satis-factory perception of it), is due to the fact that "for a thousand years the supposed or real concentration of human thought on Christian Ethics had blinded men to this struggle".[1] In the beginning, the religious-ethical Rationalism had, it is true, dethroned the prevailing Polytheism, in favour of the "one thing needful"; but afterwards in the face of the realities of the inner and outer life, as the history of the Christian Church shows, it yielded to the necessity of numerous compromises and readjustments. To-day, when Christianity is no longer the one supreme spiritual power, we see the recommencement of "the struggle between the values" or, as Weber sometimes defines it, the "struggle between the gods", for values are only an impersonal term which science, in the process of disenchantment, has introduced, to describe those great powers over life. And just as no scholar who respects the principle of objectivity would presume to decide scientifically the relative value of French and German civilisation, but would instead content himself with understanding and analysing the system of values dominant in each, though, by so doing, he would necessarily leave the important problem of life, inherent in this contrast, unsolved and even untouched—so science as a whole is not able to make a decision or to suggest a practical attitude in any struggle between ultimate values.

When, then, in this most important respect science cannot be of service, Weber presses on to the question whether it has any significance at all for determining practical conduct, not merely for technical purposes,

[1] "Wissenschaft als Beruf", S. 28.

where it is obviously of use, but as regards ultimate values. To this question an affirmative answer is given. For here, as in everything it touches, science offers clarity.

It offers, firstly, clarity with regard to the peculiar character of conduct determined by values (wert-rationales Handeln), in contrast to the other types of human behaviour. Further, it offers clarity as to the ultimate, ceaseless "struggle between the values" which man in his daily life usually does not and even will not observe, since he is for the most part inclined to content himself with compromises, and avoids what Weber calls the choice between "God" and "the Devil", and his own final decision as to which of the contending values is subject to the one and which to the other.

Now, if conduct determined by values is to be practised in human affairs, it requires certain definite means, precisely as the "zweckrationales Handeln" requires them. And science can give clarity concerning the means necessary to give effect to any specified values, while it again leaves the individual to determine whether he can accept the means which it demonstrates as essential for his purpose and, in case he cannot, it can give clarity as to how he will then decide between the "value" and the "means". For example, in political affairs—the aims for which the politician strives may be national or supernational, social, cultural, or religious—one "inevitable means" is the legitimate exercise of physical power over men, which the modern state has monopolised and on the use of which every political group and every politician counts.

Besides giving clarity as to the means, science also gives clarity as to all the consequences that can be foreseen, including the unintended accompanying consequences. Again it gives to the individual, in the case when undesirable consequences can be foreseen, the power to choose between them and the value that he wishes to pursue. Weber distinguishes two different principles according to which conduct dictated by values may be pursued: an Ethics of Faith (Gesinnungsethik), and an Ethics of Responsibility (Verantwortungsethik). By the former is meant the leading principle in the conduct of men who act only by faith, either submitting their success entirely to the will of God or, if their actions do not succeed, blaming their fellow-men; the latter term designates the leading principle in the conduct of those who feel themselves responsible also for all the foreseeable consequences of their deeds. These two principles are always at war, whatever value is pursued.

Thus, science gives clarity in different respects as to conduct dictated by values, just as in the case of "zweckrationales Handeln", but with one essential difference. The purposes of human life are for the most part settled by the nature of things and of men. But this is not the case with values. And therefore the circumstance that science can give clarity as to values brings with it the final and most essential significance. For by making man aware of the fact that a definite line of conduct can originate with inner consistency and thus with sincerity from certain ultimate valuations (either one or more), but not from others, the scientist is able to assist the individual to bring himself to account as to the final significance of his deeds. That means that science performs the task of creating clarity and strengthening the sense of responsibility, teaching man to know himself. But a person is able to achieve this, only when he refrains from urging others to adopt any particular attitude; in other words, when he respects the inner freedom of others to take on their own responsibility decisions based on the clarity they have obtained.

Thus Weber's conception, which at first appears entirely negative, is found on fuller consideration to contain a truly positive teaching, namely that of clarity which respects the freedom of others. And it seems to me to be consistent that Weber, who very seldom used the word "philosophy", asserts in this connection that specialised philosophy and the fundamental discussions of the separate sciences that are philosophical in character, endeavour to offer clarity of this kind as an aid to self-knowledge. Thus, the "philosopher" in the politician and sociologist Max Weber formulated the principle of the "Wertfreiheit" of science.

6

A third stage of post-Hegelian philosophy as reached by Husserl, Dilthey and Weber

I have endeavoured to describe Weber's conception somewhat more fully than is perhaps justified by the form of these lectures; but this seemed desirable, both because Weber's thought appears to me particularly characteristic of the stage reached in the philosophical elucidation of the principles of science, and because I hope that what has been said as to the achievements of Husserl and Dilthey can thus be supplemented and made somewhat clearer. Husserl the logician trained in mathematics, Dilthey the historian of spiritual and intellectual life, and Weber the student of the social sciences, starting from three entirely different sets of problems, seem to me to have carried the problem of philosophical knowledge a definite stage beyond the strictly epistemological investigations which were conducted by Cohen and many scientific theorists.

Without doubt, Weber's conception of the "Wertfreiheit" of science was regarded as belonging entirely to the sphere of the logical-methodological investigations which he undertook in order to gain insight into the basic principles of the social sciences. But it immediately oversteps the boundary of what may not inappropriately be termed a "science of the sciences", since it offers insight into the significance of scientific knowledge for practical action in political affairs and, in fact, in all departments of life. Here we are faced, as I think no one can doubt, with a problem that is entirely philosophical: that of the conduct of life, or as it is traditionally called: the problem of Ethics. And it seems to me very significant that there are these two elements in Weber's teaching: in the first place, very strict limits are set to the use of scientific knowledge in determining practical conduct; for the negative meaning of Weber's "Wertfreiheit" is that science can give for this no dogmatic or authoritative advice. Yet the positive meaning of such scientific knowledge, within and in spite of its limitations, is most convincingly demonstrated; for that scientific knowledge which in practical-technical respects has brought it about that instead of the "magic of the savages", modern Western civilisation has been developed, offers "clarity" in the universal sense that it awakens the feeling of responsibility and respect for the freedom of the individual.

Similarly Dilthey, who with his investigations into the basis of the Humanistic Sciences contributed to this "science of the sciences", went beyond its limits. His first achievement in this direction was that he, as the historian of spiritual and intellectual life, recognised the two different elements in philosophy, the need for Weltanschauung and for scientific proof. It was further of importance that he distinguished in his historical studies three types of Weltanschauung: naturalism, objective speculative idealism and subjective idealism of freedom, which as independent conceptions can neither be derived from each other nor combined by scientific synthesis. The final stage in the development of his thought was reached when, not content with merely observing the variety of these types and their respective absolute claims, he reflected more deeply and found historical life as a whole and personal experience (which he called "Erlebnis") to be the sources from which such Weltanschauungen originate. Thus the work of Dilthey closely resembles that of Weber in its preliminary limiting of science and in its succeeding explanation of the deeper significance of insight. Dilthey's problem, however, is different; it is not knowledge in relation to practical conduct, but knowledge in relation to Weltanschauung, that means in relation to an interpretation of existence based on a unitary and consistent attitude towards the world. Similarly Husserl with his phenomenological method has advanced beyond the sphere of the "science of the sciences" in teaching us to search behind the particular facts for the essence of phenomena and to describe their characteristic properties as adequately as possible.

The philosophical problems of the conduct of life and of the Weltanschauung, and a new and useful method of philosophical analysis, have thus been discussed by these three great scholars in a manner that satisfies the requirements of thought in the age of autonomous science. And in my opinion, it does not detract from the importance of these three pioneers to admit that they did not cross the threshold of the new philosophy towards which they led. All three were fundamentally specialised scientists, and the chief work of their lives was devoted to these subjects. And when Dilthey, a few years before his death, said with regard to the philosophical tasks which he endeavoured to accomplish: "I see the goal. If I fall by the way, I hope that my younger fellow-travellers will reach the end",[1] he was using words which might equally well describe the position of Weber or Husserl. Younger fellow-travellers must take up and carry

[1] Dilthey, *Gesammelte Werke*, Bd. v, S. 9.

43

on the tasks begun, and deeper intellectual influences must make themselves felt, if the one aim is to be realised of making clear what, in this age of autonomous science, philosophy has to accomplish for mankind.

CHAPTER II

NIETZSCHE AND KIERKEGAARD: THEIR IMPORTANCE FOR CONTEMPORARY GERMAN PHILOSOPHY

It was the purpose of the first chapter to show that Contemporary German Philosophy is not a disconnected aggregate of miscellaneous opinions, but that its course has been determined by the historical situation, which resulted from the collapse of Hegel's Philosophy and the emergence of the separate sciences. In this chapter, two thinkers of the nineteenth century, Nietzsche and Kierkegaard, will be discussed because of their determining influence.

The works of Simmel and Scheler, Jaspers and Heidegger, when compared with those of Husserl, Dilthey and Weber, reveal profound changes both in attitude and in theme: there arises a clear consciousness of the distinction between Philosophy and Science, and a tendency to attack philosophical problems in a new way, namely by abandoning the epistemological approach and starting from a fundamental phenomenon—either "Life" or "Existenz"—which is perhaps deeper, certainly more realistic, although more impervious to analysis. Such changes, though they are in part due to the personal experience and to the force of thinking of these men, are chiefly due to their

assimilation of the thought of Nietzsche and Kierkegaard. Thus the specific character of Contemporary
German Philosophy cannot be understood without an
acquaintance with the conceptions of these great
thinkers or, at least, with those that have decisively
influenced its course.

I

*Nietzsche's importance for Germany's intellectual
life as a whole and especially for Contemporary
German Philosophy*

Probably many of my readers are accustomed to regard
Nietzsche mainly as a poet, man of letters, critic, and
perhaps also as a gifted psychologist; and they may
dislike him, not only because of his ejaculatory style,
but chiefly on account of his sympathy for the
emotional and the dogma of power which becomes
apparent in his later works and which, when super-
ficially examined, has been misinterpreted as a justification of force.

It should, however, be pointed out that in Germany
during the last four or five decades no thinker has
exerted an equally far-reaching influence. And this
influence was not confined to poets and novelists like
Stefan George or Thomas Mann, nor does it depend
only upon the originality of his use of language or
upon the singular understanding of poetry and music
that permeates his entire work from the *Birth of Tragedy*,

with its distinction between the "Apollinische" and the "Dionysische", to the *Case of Wagner*. Equally one would underrate Nietzsche in judging him only by his indisputable influence on popular philosophy, however strongly this influence has been felt since the 'nineties and continues to be felt, owing to certain characteristics of his work which invite a superficial approach. For a fuller appreciation, it is necessary to realise his important achievements in the field of psychology. In Germany, at any rate, he is considered one of the greatest psychologists of the nineteenth century—to mention only one point, his discovery and description of "resentment" are very important. Moreover, what probably contributed most to the breadth of his influence was his striking critique of the false and antiquated values of the educated middle-classes, a critique by which since the 'nineties he led the rising pre-War generations to the pursuit of more genuine and realistic ideals. But none of these aspects of Nietzsche's work is important for Contemporary German Philosophy. His influence in this field arose from the fact that he raised for the first time certain problems which subsequently changed the whole philosophical outlook.

In analysing Weber's discussion of the problem of science, I have pointed out that this problem, in the form in which he treats it, was previously set by Nietzsche. In the preface to the second edition of the *Birth of Tragedy*, fifteen years after the first appearance of that work, Nietzsche says: "What I got hold of at that time, something terrible and dangerous, a problem with horns, not necessarily a bull, certainly a new problem: to-day I would say that this was the problem of science itself, science for the first time comprehended as problematical and as questionable."[1] One may well be repelled by the style of Nietzsche as a writer, but, reviewing the history of thought in the nineteenth century, one has to admit that Nietzsche as a thinker was right in this self-analysis.

His conception of "the philosopher" was also of great importance. Since the collapse of Hegel's philosophy in German intellectual life the investigator in the separate sciences had taken the place of the philosopher, and even the so-called "Fachphilosoph", or specialised philosopher, for instance the epistemologist, chose to adopt the intellectual attitude of the typical scholar. In this sense Husserl and Dilthey belong entirely, Weber, in his conscious, though not in his inner attitude, to the post-Hegelian and pre-Nietzschean era. Nietzsche was the first to recognise a fundamental distinction between the philosopher and the scientist, and his conception of the philosopher has, like his critique of the sciences, greatly influenced the leading academic philosophers starting with Simmel and Scheler.

Finally, Nietzsche recognised the significance of ultimate values for the life of the individual and of the nation. By a critique of the hitherto unquestioned ultimate values of Western civilisation he arrived long before Dilthey and Bergson at a "Philosophy of Life", of which his *Will to Power* is only one attempt towards

[1] Nietzsche, *Gesammelte Werke*, Bd. i, S. 3.

a metaphysical interpretation which moreover remained ineffective. Although Nietzsche did not achieve
a final elucidation of the philosophical problem of
values, even in its strictly logical aspect afterwards
analysed by Weber, and although by his "Philosophy
of Life", which remained in its objective contents
chiefly a naturalist theory in opposition to Christianity
and the post-Socratic belief in mind and morals, he did
no more than prepare the way for his successors. Yet
this essentially philosophical conception has exercised
so profound an influence that it cannot be neglected.

2

Nietzsche's Criticism of Science

Nietzsche's chief concern during the first period of his
work, till towards the end of his tenure of the Basel
professorship, was to awaken in young receptive minds
the sense of the inner tasks of life, that is of the need for
culture in the deepest sense, and to preserve them against
the influences both of the authoritative state which
consumes the people in its service, and of economic
life which teaches only the necessity of earning a living.
It was clear to Nietzsche that in the triumphant Germany of the 'seventies, the state and economic life
forced education more and more into their service, so
that beside them there could only exist a formal general
education, which gave a superficial polish, but nothing

to strengthen and control the inner life. These forms of education Nietzsche recognised as destructive of individuality.[1]

But when he, as a teacher of young students at a university, sought for genuine ideals to which he could direct them, he found, it is true, Greek culture, above all that of the pre-Socratic period; he found art, which with its significant and simplifying pictures of life initiated youth into what was to be expected in the future; and he found philosophers who had offered to youth, just as Schopenhauer had offered to himself, standards by which to judge the essential.[2] But among these powers he did not find science.

Nietzsche recognised as characteristic at least of the science of his time that as an autonomous study, so far from contributing to the deepening of individuality or to its strengthening for the purpose of living, it had rather, like the state and economic life, a tendency to devour the individual in its service, and to prevent him from finding himself. And it was the assumption by science of autonomy with all its consequences for

---

[1] For his fullest expression of this view see *Schopenhauer als Erzieher* (*Gesammelte Werke*, Bd. 1, S. 446 ff.) and *Über die Zukunft unserer Bildungsanstalten* (especially *Gesammelte Werke*, Bd. IX, S. 322 ff.).

[2] Nietzsche discusses Greek culture as an ideal for his own time in the *Geburt der Tragödie* and in his fragmentary work on the pre-Socratic philosophers; the significance of a creative artist in his own time, in *Richard Wagner in Bayreuth*; and the inspiring influence of a true philosopher in *Schopenhauer als Erzieher*.

human life and individuality, which formed the starting-point of his criticism.[1]

The philosopher and the artist must, no doubt, be for long periods isolated from the world, as is the scientist. Nevertheless, from a more profound point of view, they remain connected with life through their work. But the student of an autonomous science, according to Nietzsche, separates himself from life not only temporarily and so to speak technically, but, as far as possible, finally. He does not share in the deep suffering which in various forms, caused for instance by death, struggle, injustice, necessarily belongs to human life; he does not revolt against it or try to cope with it, but remains indifferent and cold, as if his life belonged to another world; and if in a leisure hour he happens upon such speculations, then they present for him, who in science deals only with problems of knowledge, merely further problems.

Such an attitude of the scientist to real life would be justified, if thought and research could realise his first and highest hope: to penetrate to the deepest funda-

[1] Nietzsche's fundamental negative criticism of science is brought forward in his earlier works; from *Menschliches Allzumenschliches* to *Fröhliche Wissenschaft* he assumes towards science a more positive attitude, and in his later works he deals only incidentally with the problem of science. His negative criticism is to be found mainly in the *Geburt der Tragödie*, especially Chapters XIII–XV and XVIII, in *Schopenhauer als Erzieher*, Kap. 6 (*Gesammelte Werke*, Bd. I, S. 453 ff.), in *Nutzen und Nachteil der Geschichte für das Leben*, Chapters IV–IX, and in *David Friedrich Strauss, der Bekenner und Schriftsteller*.

mentals of existence and, with the help of such knowledge, to satisfy, if only in the distant future, the outward and inward needs of living. Nietzsche had no doubt that such a belief in the unlimited power of knowledge inspired the great founders of the theoretical approach, Socrates and Plato, giving to Socrates the strength to meet his death calmly and trusting in the might of truth and giving to Plato the enthusiasm to proclaim the significance of knowledge for the domination of Good in the world. But Nietzsche was equally aware that this belief had revealed itself progressively more and more to be an illusion, especially since Kant's criticism of the knowledge which is attained through understanding. The student of the autonomous sciences, very remote from any hope that his knowledge will bring about the rule of the Good and cure the sufferings of humanity, has long ago given up even the attempt to understand by his investigations Being as a whole. Instead he contents himself with discovering separate phenomena, which in his investigation he artificially isolates from the whole of existence, and with finding in them separate unrecognised relationships.

But even with such restrictions, if the scientist admits his limitations science has a certain relative significance, and Nietzsche, of course, highly esteemed the qualities of a sound scholarship and the intellectual power of scepticism and criticism which the scholar's training can develop. But autonomous science can no longer claim to be what it imagined itself before Nietzsche's criticism: the highest intellectual achievement in the whole history of the Western mind.

This misguided claim involved the training of young scholars and the cultural life of the nation in grave danger, to which Nietzsche sought to direct the attention of his contemporaries. Science had, as a consequence of its desire for progress, become a factory by which, so to speak, objective truth was continually being produced and thrown on to the market, without regard to the relative importance of what was discovered or to the extent to which young people were exhausted in a premature, artificially forced rush of production.

By this process, in the historical and philological sciences, as Nietzsche has pointed out in his famous treatise *On the Advantage and Disadvantage of History for Life*, there was a dominating tendency to investigate all objectively ascertainable facts, which tendency had destructive influences on the development of individuality and of real culture. In opposition to this, Nietzsche emphasises that historical research is in the deepest sense fruitful and alive only when it is pursued for a vital purpose; and he distinguishes three different ways in which history can serve, and has served life. It can strengthen the ties with the past, when one reflects with piety on one's origin, family or nation (antiquarische Historie); it can inspire and encourage the strivings of the active man by reminding him of the great achievements of former times (monumentalische Historie); or it can dissolve a traditional conception by subjecting it to the tribunal of critical thought (kritische Historie).

With reference to the historical and humanistic studies, Nietzsche put the following questions to his contemporaries, whether history must not above all relate to life and serve it, and whether life, with the possibility of culture being realised in mature personalities, is not to be preferred to the cult of autonomous science. This point of view found no hearing in the 'seventies, 'eighties and 'nineties, at a time when German scientists were still dominated by the idea of scientific progress, and, as has already been said, it began to be understood in its true significance only shortly before the World War. Though Nietzsche here as elsewhere did not sum up his statements in a final form, these fundamental problems were thus set for his successors: (1) What is the significance of this method of seeking truth called science, when apprehended in its unique historical form, since its origin in Greece? and (2) Does the scientist not need a deeper, more vital motivation of his activities than the mere urge to search for unknown phenomena?

3

Nietzsche's Conception of the Philosopher

Thus Nietzsche, in an age when science was regarded as the highest achievement of humanity, called in question its fundamental significance. At the same time, in a generation which, although familiar with epistemological problems, had forgotten wherein philosophy consists, he reawakened a sense of its true significance.

Here Nietzsche's thought had a twofold importance: (1) In contrast to scientific philosophy with its analysis of individual problems, he points to its universal tasks —the importance of philosophy for human conduct and for the interpretation of existence. (2) He does not consider philosophy to be a superpersonal study like science, a study to which each student can make his limited contribution. Rather, he assigns a decisive significance to the individual true philosopher who, moved by his love of wisdom, shapes his life according to his philosophical thought and creates in his work a new interpretation of existence. Although such a philosopher rarely exists, whenever he does occur he proves to be of supreme importance to his fellowmen.

If to some persons this now appears self-evident, the reminder of the extreme significance of the individual true philosopher was necessary at a time when interest in philosophy was so little alive, and the scholar was considered so much the standard of all intellectual activity as in the second half of the nineteenth century; that is, it was necessary if philosophy was to have a future at all comparable to that of the sciences. It was this emphasis on the individual philosopher which subsequently influenced German thinkers such as Simmel, Scheler, Klages, Jaspers and Heidegger; and it must be clearly realised if the whole development of modern German philosophy is to be accurately understood.

Philosophy in Nietzsche's sense is "love of wisdom", the philosopher is the "friend of wisdom".[1] To Nietzsche

[1] Cf. *Gesammelte Werke*, Bd. x, S. 295–6; and with reference to the following, the two fragments "Philosophie in Bedrängnis" (*Gesammelte Werke*, Bd. x, S. 285–313) and "Wissenschaft und Weisheit im Kampfe" (*Gesammelte Werke*, Bd. x, 216–37).

these expressions are more than a mere translation of the Greek terms, since the use of those as part of a traditional terminology seemed to him to denote a lack of the essential quality of philosophising. Thus he criticised his contemporaries as mere eclectics or concerned only with the detail of epistemological problems, or restricted to the meticulous expounding of the great philosophical thought of the past; for to him, "love of wisdom" is the true criterion for the philosophising individual, and in this sense Schopenhauer alone among recent thinkers had fulfilled this high demand.[1]

The first consequence of such a fundamental desire for wisdom is that the individual has to philosophise for himself alone with such seriousness and sincerity, as though no one had previously philosophised and he himself had to discover all truth and find his own standards for the conduct of life. Only in this way, Nietzsche is convinced, can an individual eventually become a philosopher. All other ways of philosophising he considers bound to fail and characterises as a trade in thought (Denkwirtschaft).[2] In this sense he denounces not only "Sophistry", making its inherited technique

[1] Apart from scattered negative criticisms of philosophers to be found in almost all of his works from the earliest to the latest, Nietzsche's own conception of a philosopher is expressed in his early work *Schopenhauer als Erzieher* and the same subject is treated very definitely and suggestively in "Wir Gelehrte", a chapter of his late work *Jenseits von Gut und Böse*. Besides these two descriptions, Nietzsche in the person of Zarathustra has set forth his ideal of a prophetic philosopher.

[2] *Gesammelte Werke*, Bd. x, S. 302–4.

of thinking a matter for bargaining, but also the usual school-philosophy which, starting with already established problems and doctrines, handles them as independent subject-matter to be investigated within its own sphere. In opposition to such prevailing tendencies, Nietzsche maintains that philosophical thought should not be stretched on to a ready-made framework of thinking nor be dealt with as a doctrine or a set of objective problems. For philosophical thought can be of true significance only in so far as it succeeds in clarifying the problem of existence in an original manner, new for every generation.

According to Nietzsche, the philosopher differs essentially from the artist in that he cannot fulfil himself in his work alone. The life of the great artist alternates between periods of creative work in which he realises his subjective experience in symbolical images, and phases of barren every-day existence; compared with the importance of the accomplished work, his life appears insignificant. But to the true philosopher the application of his principles is of such account that it permeates and shapes even his every-day existence with a rigour akin to that which is found in the life of a saint. But unlike the saint, the philosopher must not content himself with modelling life according to his ideals. While the former spends himself entirely in his devotion to the purification of the inner self, the latter, undeterred by his own deficiencies, yet with rigid self-criticism, must present and argue in a consistent manner his insight into the facts of existence. Thus, in the search for truth, the true philosopher, moved by his love of wisdom, is confronted with two distinct tasks: he has to conduct his own life in a philosophical manner and to create in his work a new interpretation of existence.[1] This demand for a new standard of philosophising places Nietzsche beside Kierkegaard, and distinguishes his conception of philosophy fundamentally from that of Dilthey, though the work of both can be included under the heading "Philosophy of Life".

The manner in which a philosopher conducts his life and in which he has reshaped his character is of such great importance because it is here that the effectiveness of philosophical thought becomes most easily apparent. To Nietzsche, therefore, the life of a philosopher is not a private affair, as is the life of most other persons, including great artists, but it is an essential part of his philosophical work; in fact its first realisation, the genuine character of which may show itself as an instructive example, independent of the argument of his system of thought. In this sense, Nietzsche as early as in *Thoughts out of Season* refers to Schopenhauer not as the author of a philosophical system, but as an "Educator". He thereby emphasises the exemplary value of certain qualities inherent in a philosophical character, such as integrity, tranquillity, consistency (Redlichkeit, Heiterkeit, Beständigkeit).[2] Throughout his work Nietzsche regards integrity as

[1] Cf. *Gesammelte Werke*, Bd. x, S. 296. But this conception of the philosopher runs through Nietzsche's whole work, though it is seldom as clearly expressed as here.

[2] *Schopenhauer als Erzieher*, Kap. 2 (*Gesammelte Werke*, Bd. i, S. 398 ff.).

the supreme human virtue and as of particular importance to a philosopher who will not deceive himself
about the significance and the tasks of our human
existence, and who will not pretend to himself or to
others. Further, tranquillity is not a peculiarity of the
original temperament of a philosopher, but a trait that
gradually develops as he faces and overcomes adversity;
this tranquillity shows itself in the manner in which,
unlike other men, he moves through life with surety
and determination, and in the simple and clear expression
of his opinions. Finally, consistency is manifest, because the philosopher throughout his life obeys his
most profound impulses and does not submit to the
external forces of life, by which most people are
governed and consumed. Such consistency in the life
of a true philosopher, which can often be observed in
the decisions of his youth, throughout his work and in
all his actions, is a powerful indication of the genuine
character of his philosophy, and serves as a reminder of
the possibilities open for the conduct of life.

It must be always borne in mind, however, that the
main task for the philosopher is not the search for an
adequate manner of living, but the ceaseless attempt to
enlighten himself and others concerning the problem of
existence. For, throughout his life, the true philosopher
is conscious of the whole of existence in its incomprehensibility, and he does not rest until he has succeeded
in a new interpretation. To use Nietzsche's metaphor,
he follows this task undistracted, as Hamlet follows the
ghost.

Philosophical interpretation is based upon a type of

knowledge different from that of the scientist. The philosopher has not confined himself to a definite sphere of knowledge, and he is not governed by the desire to explore it in full detail. But his selection of subjects for investigation is determined by a standard of what is most worthy of investigation. And on the other hand, the philosopher is aided not only by his rational understanding, but also by a controlled imagination which in an instant enables him to realise a multitude of possibilities.

Moreover, going beyond the objectivity of the scientist, he throws himself into his studies with the whole strength of his personality, since he is not content to reach a survey of the knowledge of his time, but desires to gain a convincing attitude towards previous interpretations of existence and towards the problem of existence itself. For convincing interpretation of the whole of existence is not possible as a comprehensive exposition in the scientific sense. It cannot be achieved unless the philosopher, after serious self-examination, has reached his final conclusions about Life, and has in the face of the many senseless facts become clear as to where the positive values of human existence are to be found.

By his interpretation of existence and by the example of a philosophical conduct of life the philosopher exerts his influence on the individual and on his time.

True philosophy has the power of concentrating the individual. It gives an integrated view with which to interpret the separate events and emotions of life. As was known in earlier times but almost forgotten in the nineteenth century, philosophy provides for the individual a higher intellectual standard and a truer education than he could achieve in any other way.

For the intellectual life of his time the philosopher is important, in Nietzsche's words, as a "physician of culture". Because of the insight he has gained, he will, in his ceaseless search for truth, attempt to correct all the tendencies which are likely to exert barbarous, brutalising and stupefying influences.

Thus, in the course of history, philosophy has been confronted with a variety of tasks. In the beginning, it was necessary to overcome the mythical tendencies in thought and to strengthen the longing for truth against the play of free poetical imagination, while on the contrary, in modern times the unlimited desire for detailed knowledge had to be curbed. Further, at times, it was important to break up by philosophical scepticism the rigid dogmatism in religion, custom and science, while at other times the trend towards blind worldliness had to be exposed. For while beginning by philosophising for himself alone, the true philosopher will in the end feel himself responsible for the intellectual life of his time. And although it is obviously impossible for a philosopher to create a new civilisation, he will always be concerned to preserve the true significance of existing culture, he will moderate excesses and, in times of barbarism, he will attempt to prepare the foundations for a future civilisation.

Again Nietzsche's assertion must be remembered that such a philosopher rarely exists. The influential factors in his surroundings may be unfavourable, or his personal equipment may be inadequate for the perfect completion of his work; he may fail from loneliness or friendlessness; he may despair of the accessibility of truth or the attainment of perfection of character; or else he may tire too soon as an investigator, especially now that the structure of science has grown to such vast proportions; there is also the chance that he may become too firmly fixed in one specialised field, and so be unable to achieve a general survey; or his conscience may be too sensitive, or he himself too modest, ever to have confidence to pass judgment even on the sciences, let alone on life and life-values.[1]

Nevertheless, according to Nietzsche's conviction, a man is a philosopher only when, out of a genuine love of wisdom, he perseveres in his life and work in spite of all difficulties and distractions. To such concentration is due the success of the great philosophers of the past down to Hegel and Schopenhauer.

4

Nietzsche's " Philosophy of Life"

The importance of Nietzsche for Contemporary Philosophy is not confined to his criticism of Science and to his emphasis on the true Philosopher. These are merely two of his efforts to correct, as a philosopher, one particular excess and one particular deficiency in the

[1] *Schopenhauer als Erzieher*, Kap. 3 (*Gesammelte Werke*, Bd. I, S. 404 ff.); *Jenseits von Gut und Böse*, Aph. 205 ff. (*Gesammelte Werke*, Bd. VII, S. 146 ff.).

intellectual life of his time. But his main importance is based upon the attempt to give, in his "Philosophy of Life", a new interpretation of existence.

To understand the fragmentary character of this interpretation, it must be realised that Nietzsche arrived at this conception only late in life, having lost the hope of reawakening humanistic culture, and having passed through a long period of critical search. Not until the years during which *Zarathustra* was written (1883–85) did he conceive the thoughts that formed the basis for his own philosophy. And it was only during the period of less than four years between the finishing of *Zarathustra* and the outbreak of his mental disease that he began to work out his ideas in detail as a preparation for his intended future work.

This "Philosophy of Life" is founded upon a comprehensive critique of the *History of Western Civilisation*.

In his later work, Nietzsche reached the conclusion not only that science in its autonomy has a very limited significance and that the ideal of a humanistic culture is impossible of realisation, but also that the highest values in religion, morals and philosophy, after dominating and shaping European life for two thousand years, had begun in his time to lose their power. A feeling of general insecurity, and the more conscious tendencies of scepticism and pessimism, were spreading rapidly, and were the forerunners of a still more serious evil, Nihilism, which Nietzsche considered inevitable. With this insight into the character of his times, and convinced that events should not be allowed merely to

take their course, he grasped the necessity of a re-
flective analysis of the origin of these highest values
and of the reason for the coming of Nihilism, in order,
if it were at all feasible, to find a way through this development, which he considered so threatening to
European civilisation. Only with this explanation as a
background can we understand Nietzsche's early critique of the world-view presented by Socrates and Plato,
and his subsequent critique of Christianity; isolated,
these do not appear in their full significance. This can
only be seen in connection with his historical theory
that the old interpretations of existence, which had
dominated European life since Socrates and which,
through the medium of Christianity, provided the clue
to European life in the Middle Ages and in early modern
times, had become outworn and henceforth would be
useless as guidance for the future. In this sense the
historical part of his philosophical work is contained in
the aphorisms of the first and second volumes of the
Will to Power, namely "European Nihilism" and "The
Critique of previously accepted Fundamental Values",
together with many less conscious preparatory analyses
written from the *Birth of Tragedy* onwards.

And thus at the end of his life Nietzsche became a
"critical historian" who tried to dispose of a past in
order to prepare room for the future.

But Nietzsche's intention was not to be a critic: his
historical analysis of philosophy, Christianity, and
morals was only to be the starting-point for his positive
search. Had he been able to find support and satisfaction in one of the traditional ideals, he would not

have advanced to his philosophy of life. Realising, however, that we cannot believe in the existence, behind this real world, of another "true" or "good" or "divine" world, conceptions which alternatively or combined held the place of supreme values till the beginning of the nineteenth century, and which we are now inclined to regard as flights from reality and as weaknesses, he found himself confronted anew with the old questions: how is the real world to be interpreted theoretically? and in what practical attitude to life are we to find a new meaning? These problems led him from his critical investigations into the supreme values of Western civilisation to his constructive philosophy of life.

To Nietzsche, as to Dilthey, Life was the ultimate reality, the one object of his meditations after he had lost the faith of his youth that genius and culture should be the highest aims of human society. But, unlike Dilthey, Nietzsche did not reflect on the tension between science and Weltanschauung, and on the origin of the variety of Weltanschauungen in historical life. As a psychologist he tried rather to understand the driving forces in the minds of individual historical characters, their strength and weakness, their genuineness or self-deceit, their vital power (which Nietzsche calls "Wohlgeratenheit") or decadence. To analyse the unconscious motive forces of the mind was the leading impulse in his psychological research.

Generalising by degrees, he later more and more inclined to assume the "will to power" as the all-determining principle in the individual, in society, in the development of the mind, in art and even in organic and in inorganic nature. This attempt, only published as a posthumous work, towards a theoretical interpretation of the world was, I think, undertaken with the idea of pointing out, against the threat of rising Nihilism, new valuations which might spring from a return to earthly life and to all fruitful forms of activity. For by his research Nietzsche was led to the view that only that life was worth living which develops the strength and integrity to withstand the unavoidable sufferings and misfortunes of existence without becoming hardened and embittered and without flying into an imaginary world.[1]

Nietzsche, as I have said, only sketched, and did not fully work out, his philosophy of life. Though from his *Gay Science* onwards it becomes clearer and clearer, it always remains a beginning. But, in contrast to the philosophical synthesis of Fechner and Lotze and to the epistemological and methodological attempts which form the starting-point for Husserl and Dilthey, it was a beginning in the sense of which Nietzsche spoke when he said that the philosopher must interpret anew the whole of existence, determine anew "the measure, currency and weight of things". Nietzsche's attempted philosophy of life was the first full expression of the fact that, with Hegel's philosophy, the old philoso-

---

[1] Nietzsche's philosophy of life which first appears in his conception of the "Dionysische" in the *Geburt der Tragödie* can be traced in various works, especially in those written after the *Zarathustra*, and is most completely expressed in the aphorisms contained in volumes III and IV of the *Will to Power*.

phising had come to an end and a new philosophising was beginning, even though it had not yet attained any clear or definite form. The difference between Hegel's and Nietzsche's conception of philosophy is illustrated by the way in which they symbolise their philosophy. Hegel compares his philosophy, which generalising from remembrance summarises the past, to the owl of Minerva, which takes to flight in the twilight. Nietzsche compares his philosophy, which relates to the future, to the lightning which, flashing at night, brightens for a moment the darkness.

5
Nietzsche's Influence on some later Thinkers

It is only natural that the powerful personality of Nietzsche with his revolutionary appeal and his new problems should in due course make itself felt in academic as well as in non-academic life. All the more so, because from the 'nineties many people were acutely aware of the need for a rejuvenescence of our stereotyped forms of life. It will suffice to mention the youth-movement, the Stefan-George-Kreis, the rising of expressionism with Franz Marc and others, Naumann and the social reformers around him and the emancipation movement. Especially because of the hardships endured during and after the War, many intellectuals were swept along in the general excitement in which despair was mingled with feverish hope.

For philosophy, the influence of Nietzsche, combined with the effects of the War and the socialist revolution, brought many disadvantages, but also some gain. It led to a sterile sensationalism, to the rise of strange sects, whose leaders claimed to show the true way to wisdom. Of these perhaps the most remarkable are the Anthroposophen founded by Rudolph Steiner, and the followers of Graf Keyserling. On the whole, there was a dangerous spread of pseudo-education, a lowering of scientific standards, and a decline in thoroughness and precision of thinking. On the other hand, during the first years of this century and still more after the War, a few people appeared with a keen sense of the driving forces in life, of the problems of the day and of the task of the philosopher, apart from the mere provision of the foundations for the various sciences. More or less influenced by Nietzsche, they were not philosophers in his exemplary sense, but they realised a new and more independent philosophical attitude and produced work which was more focused in contemporary events, more concerned with the attempt to impress a meaning on them, more directed towards a philosophy of life, than that of the schools of academic philosophy. As representative of this type of thinking, I wish to describe briefly the work of Simmel, Scheler, Spengler and Klages who, though they developed independently of each other, are all characteristic of this tendency.

Simmel, who was the first academic exponent of this new type of thought, taught at Berlin University till the beginning of the War. Characteristic of him was a special passionate kind of thinking, in which he, considering various objects, from the handle of a pot to the work of Michelangelo, "lowered a sounding-line into the depth of ultimate spiritual significance". But, in so doing, he was not aiming at a consistent philosophical system. For he considered as a prejudice, which contradicted the "functional" rather than "substantial" essence of philosophy, the common belief that the actual variety of such thinking could be reduced to order in a unitary manner. He was equipped with an unusual agility of thought and a wealth of ideas, and it was this which made his "philosophy of relativism" especially productive. He developed in his early period ideas similar to the pragmatism soon afterwards expounded by James. He devoted extensive works to investigations in the field of moral science, sociology, philosophical problems of economics, of history, of civilisation and of art. But he exercised his most lasting influence through a new type of biography of selected creative personalities. In this way he analysed the work of Kant, Goethe and Rembrandt and in another study he brought out the significance of Schopenhauer's and Nietzsche's philosophies for the life of their time. By focusing his attention on the essential qualities of the work of an individual, he tried to seize the particular significance of his production, thus freeing himself from the usual procedure in biography, psychology, aesthetics, history of art and philosophy. His last and most profound work consists of studies preparatory to a metaphysics of Life (entitled *Lebensanschauung*). Here he tried to formulate

its fundamental characteristic, to be at the same time
"more life and more than life" (Mehr-Leben und Mehr-
als-Leben). He further expounds the transcendental
significance of the origin of ideas in human life. He
then interprets death as inherent in life, and to this
relates various historical conceptions of immortality.
All this leads up to the formation of the concept of the
"law of the individual" (individuelles Gesetz), by
which he tries to extend Kant's *Ethics*. In this conception is to be found the principle underlying his
various biographies, and it prepares the way for certain
further developments in contemporary philosophy.

Scheler, a man of extreme intellectual restlessness, is
important chiefly because, while he was absorbed in,
and gave expression to, successive currents in the
thought of his age, he at the same time, owing to his
fuller interest in human life, widened and deepened the
hitherto strictly scientific phenomenological researches,
and in both ways he continually sought to attain for
himself a philosophical Weltanschauung. In 1915, in
his *Genius des Krieges*, he endeavoured to set forth the
principles underlying war; after the War he placed his
hopes in the Catholic religion which formed the background of *Vom Ewigen im Menschen* (1921); while in
his last sceptical, atheistical period, after 1923, he came to
a standpoint similar to that of Freud and Klages; with
them he conceived the instincts as the powerful and
driving forces in life, whereas consciousness, which is
peculiar to humanity and from which originate three
sorts of knowledge, practical, cultural and religious, is
by itself powerless. Apart from these writings, which

were responses to the immediate problems of his time, his early phenomenological investigations on the "feelings of sympathy" and the "ethics of material values" are of permanent worth, as are also some of the analyses in his late book, *Die Wissensformen und die Gesellschaft*. Moreover, he was the first to bring forward, towards the end of his life, the demand for a "philosophical anthropology", that is, a philosophical enquiry into the nature of man in order to make clear the basis of philosophising.

Spengler, who did not belong to any academic school, developed his understanding of individuals, of historical eras and of types of civilisation under the influence of Nietzsche. He had a special capacity for seeing the peculiar characteristics and the weaknesses of the last century and of our present time. These gifts secured, immediately after the War, an extraordinary success for his work *The Decline of the West*. Soon, however, its arbitrary interpretation of world-history, as comprising a succession of individual civilisations each of which developed and grew old like a living organism, and its dogmatic way of refusing to recognise the uncertainty of the future, were seen to be serious defects.

Klages, who also stood outside academic life, is more important, although in the end he developed a strange and certainly one-sided metaphysics of life, in which he considers the human mind as antagonistic to, and destructive of, the human soul and human existence as a whole. A definite achievement of his earlier period is to be found in his investigations on graphology, in which subject he was the first to bring out some scientific principles; likewise his book *Principles of Character-Analysis*, describing a variety of phenomena, generally considered to belong to the realm of poetry, is unusually instructive, though coloured by his metaphysical antithesis between the primitive life-spending impulse and the intellectual egoistic impulse of self-preservation. He was strongly influenced by the Romantic Movement, by Nietzsche and by Stefan George, and must be given credit for having renewed the interest of his contemporaries in the forgotten Naturphilosophie of the Romantic period, especially that of Carus, and in Bachofen, the eminent historian of the "Mutterrecht", and for having elucidated Nietzsche's great contribution to psychology.

6

Kierkegaard's Personality and Work

The second thinker who has had an important influence on German philosophy of to-day is the Dane, Sören Kierkegaard. Although his works were published in the 'forties and 'fifties of the last century, thirty years before those of Nietzsche, his influence began to be profoundly felt in Germany only much later, shortly before the War, when the body of his works became accessible in translation. But the extent of his influence never, I think, approached that of Nietzsche. Besides largely determining the conduct of life for a certain number of individuals, he exercised a decisive influence on Protestant theology, especially through the medium of Karl Barth,[1] on philosophy and on some aspects of the psychology of mind. But the influence of Kierkegaard, it seems to me, passed its zenith some time ago. It was at its height in the years immediately after the War, when Germany, defeated and poor, tried to rebuild her life from inner sources. Nevertheless, it is due to his work that the two leading philosophers of the last decade, Jaspers and Heidegger, attained to their most fundamental principle, and thus contemporary philosophy, like Protestant theology, received from Kierkegaard its decisive impulse.

The development of Sören Kierkegaard's work was, in my opinion, determined by three influences—primarily and most deeply of all by Protestant Christianity. In 1830, Kierkegaard, at the age of seventeen, began the study of theology. The further he progressed, the more his writings expressed his sense of the difficulty of becoming a Christian in the true sense; and in the year 1855, shortly before his early death, he made an open attack on the Danish National Church in a pamphlet entitled *The Moment* ("Der Augenblick"). Secondly, he was affected by the Romantic views on life and art

[1] Barth recognised in Kierkegaard the antithesis of the liberal Schleiermacher. For Schleiermacher's interpretation of religion centred in the human feeling of complete dependence, whilst Kierkegaard's conception was that of a supremely real God, whom man could approach only in "fear and trembling", and who revealed himself through his "elect", through his Son Christ and through "apostles".

that attracted him as an artistically gifted young man, although in the end they failed to satisfy the deep earnestness of his nature. The third important influence was Hegel's speculative philosophy, from which he obtained his mental training, but which, when considered in its content and its importance for the conduct of life, seemed to him abstract; and compared with the reality of an individual human life, true to its faith amidst all temptations, it appeared to him vapid, arrogant and little better than trickery.

However, Kierkegaard's importance for philosophy does not consist chiefly in the criticism of Hegel which is to be found in his *Philosophical Fragments* and especially in his still more important *Unscientific Postscript*, important though these books may be for the criticism of Hegel since 1830. Among the many attempts at criticism directed against Hegel since the 'thirties and 'forties of the last century, beginning with those of Schelling in his old age and of Feuerbach and since then frequently undertaken, which have brought forward possible, and sometimes weighty, objections to Hegel's philosophy, only two have succeeded in achieving a penetrating criticism directed against this philosophy as a whole, by operating with positively conceived principles—those of Karl Marx and of Kierkegaard. But this criticism, though a great achievement in itself, is not the main reason for the interest taken in Kierkegaard by contemporary German philosophers.

His importance is rather due to the tension in his mind between two opposing forces: his sensitiveness

74

towards the world especially in its most sublime aspects of love, music and poetry, and his religious restlessness, akin to that of Augustine and Pascal. This tension is increased by Kierkegaard's absolute integrity, which he, like Nietzsche, regarded as the supreme, and even as the only, virtue and as the origin of truthfulness and of all search after truth. Kierkegaard's inner conflict became the more evident as he demanded of himself not only clearness about reality, but unity in the conduct of his life, and it became actually serious and important, when, at the age of twenty-eight, he broke off his engagement with Regine Olsen. This event opened that phase of Kierkegaard's life, the fourteen years of his writings and sermons, in which he brought himself to a decision between the opposing forces in his inner struggles.

Since, so far as I am aware, Kierkegaard's works are not yet accessible in English, I should like to state that he seems to us in Germany one of the most remarkable psychologists of all time, in depth, if not in breadth, superior to Nietzsche, and in penetration comparable only to Dostoievsky. Like Dostoievsky, who did not confine himself to the narration of character-development, in the manner of Balzac, Flaubert and Tolstoi, Kierkegaard in *Either-Or*, in *Stages on the Way of Life*, and more profoundly and consciously in *The Conception of Anxiety* and *Sickness unto Death*, with its portrayal of the different forms of despair, discloses the ultimate potentialities of the human soul. And just as Dostoievsky in the last twenty years of his life had but one question before his mind, how to meet and overcome the imminent danger of Nihilism, so Kierke-gaard was perpetually occupied with the problem of how the modern man, who has come to find his life in this world, can nevertheless attain to inner peace. And as Dostoievsky pursued this aim in his novels, so Kierkegaard followed it in monologues or dialogues of imaginary people who expounded their views on life. In spite of the philosophical nature of his work, it is so poetical that a sympathetic German biographer[1] recently described him as "the *poet* of religion".

"Poet of *religion.*" In spite of his psychological penetration, his poetic imagination and his philoso-phical desire to understand life through and through, it must always be remembered that the important question in all his writings is how to become a Christian. His purpose was not to glorify the Christian faith, nor to attack the Danish and European Churches which he considered Christian only in name; but to emphasise the difficulty of man, with his natural passions and his longing for happiness and reduced, as he is, to a mere unit in the membership of the modern state, to attain the fortitude of religion with the eternal responsibility before God, and thus become truly Christian. Of this difficulty and of what such a Christian life might mean, Kierkegaard gives a philosophical analysis which is unique; and I am inclined to believe that, if the history of the philosophy of Christianity were to be written, his interpretation would be ranked among the few great efforts to conceive Christianity as it originally

[1] Martin Thust, *Sören Kierkegaard, der Dichter des Religiösen,* München, 1931.

was, an attempt made formerly by Augustine and by Luther. But there is this difference, that Kierkegaard undertook his task in the middle of the nineteenth century, when the secularisation of the European peoples was far advanced, that, unlike Luther, he aimed at an ultimate philosophical clarification, and that he was equipped with a deeper knowledge of the human soul than was Augustine. If, after the War, German Protestant Christianity experienced an unexpected revival, it was above all due to the writings of Kierkegaard.

But, although this work may have the greatest importance for Protestant theology and the regeneration of Christianity, and may have had a considerable influence, opposing and supplementing that of Freud and Klages, on the psychology of mind, it may well be asked: of what significance is it for philosophy, for which neither Christianity nor psychology is essential? How can Kierkegaard be important for contemporary philosophy, if, as I have said, he was from first to last a writer whose only purpose was to direct attention to Christianity?

The answer is: on account of his conception of the "Existenz of the Individual" and his insight into the fundamental difference between "Existential Thinking" and "Abstract Speculation". When Heidegger to-day gives an "Existential" analysis of human existence, in order to discuss the original philosophical question of Being in a new and more satisfactory way, and when Jaspers describes one of the fundamental ways of philosophising as the elucidation of "Existenz", both have been greatly influenced by Kierkegaard. In contrast to Dilthey and Nietzsche, Simmel and Klages, they are thinking about Existenz and not about Life. Now, what does Existenz mean, and what is Existential Thinking? They may be explained by an example taken from Kierkegaard, his conception of "Choice".

7
Kierkegaard's Thoughts on "Choice"

The meaning of "choice" for man was expounded by Kierkegaard in his first work, entitled *Either-Or*. The book consists of two parts, in which the reader becomes acquainted with the papers of an aesthetic person *A* and of a moral person *B* who are assumed to be acquainted with each other. *A* is the pure type of romantic, imaginative, artistic, ironical character, intimately acquainted with music and drama, sparkling in his paradoxical aphorisms and monological essays which centre round the erotic as the seductive influence in life and art. But at bottom he is melancholy, restless and desperate, longing for pleasure but not enjoying it, suffering from life and pondering upon it in self-torturing reflection. *B*, on the other hand, has found happiness in marriage and in his profession. He thinks he can understand *A*, and by his sympathy for him tries to make him sensible of his state of self-destruction, in order by his appeal to induce him to choose consciously and freely between the two fundamental possibilities, either being swept along by life in its manifold moods, or steering a firm course through it.

For such a choice as that to which the moral *B* is urging the aesthetic *A*, it is not particularly significant that one should choose a definite thing, or even that one's choice should be objectively right; but that he who chooses should do so with his whole complete being, out of a fundamental earnestness. It is a choice which, as the moral man *B*, and probably Kierkegaard himself, supposed, no one can escape from making; at any rate, no adult person who wishes to "exist", that is to conduct, and not merely to be driven by, life.

Such a "choice" might be described thus. It may start from an absolute despair and repentance, which is followed by a moment in which the individual isolates himself from the whole of the rest of the world. In this isolation he breaks completely with his previous life, and this break first leads up to the individual's arriving at a true and responsible realisation of his life; he then turns back to the world, accepting his own past, the people around him and his own condition of life. In this new phase he becomes clear to himself and communicable to his friends. One could draw the process of such a "choice" in much greater detail, stressing this or that feature, or emphasising with the moral *B* (and with Kierkegaard), for whom he speaks, its relevance for life. But what I wish here to bring out is the peculiar difficulty of calling anyone's attention to such a strange and important phenomenon as this "choice".

For such a choice can neither be described in its

true character by psychological methods, nor can it be made the object of an ethical appeal. It cannot be adequately described psychologically, because it must be brought about by an inner attitude of the individual as a whole, while psychological analysis implies that the object to be analysed is something different from the conscious thinking which makes the analysis. Nor can such a choice be demanded ethically, since the resolve to make it, if it comes at all, must come spontaneously from an inner impulse of the individual. An objectively cogent categorical imperative for the "choice" cannot be given.

Nevertheless, a man who has once made the "choice" will not only know himself to be definitely changed from what he was before, but possibly will also want to induce to such a choice a friend whom he realises to be in a similar initial frame of mind.

But how can he do this? Obviously only in the same way as Socrates, who, by his maieutic method of dialectic, tried to bring about philosophic "births". Socrates, though himself a philosopher, cannot by definite teaching induce others to philosophise. Philosophising requires every individual to think for himself. And this thinking for oneself is awakened by Socrates' way of questioning, keeping silence, being astonished, not understanding. By these means he calls the attention of his pupils to the activity which they themselves must choose to pursue.

Kierkegaard's "choice of oneself" is a process into which it is much more difficult to be initiated by another person than thinking for oneself.

THOUGHTS ON "CHOICE"

Thinking for oneself starts as an *activity* from within, but *choosing* oneself is an inner *attitude* of the individual *towards himself as a whole*. The choice of oneself is, metaphorically speaking, to "leap over an abyss". Whenever in life this leap has to be taken I have to take it for myself, and similarly other people have to take it for themselves, it can neither be taken by deputy nor with anybody's assistance.

Let us consider, then, a man who has experienced the necessity of such a choice—a subjective necessity and a choice that is of relevance only to the individual himself or to those in close relationship to him—and who, aware that he could not escape, has effected the "choice". What can he do to help another out of his difficulty?

An empirical, psychological discussion of his own act of choosing is useless; the other man has to be roused to choose himself. Description of the actual "choice", though it may be perfect, is for this purpose vain. And to demand the choice directly is impossible, for everything depends upon the inner impulse.

There is only one thing to be done: To transform in imagination one's own realised choice into a possibility that has reference to the future, and to call attention from one's remembrance to the possibility of the choice of oneself in its absolute significance. To call attention to possibilities of Existenz may seem very little; but anything more than this would be to interfere by force with the freedom of another, the maintenance of which freedom is the presupposition of all Existenz-possibilities.

In this way the man *B*, who has made his choice, calls the attention of *A*, wrapt-up in his melancholy, to the possibility of choice and its importance for life. In such a way of calling attention, Kierkegaard himself, in the hundreds of pages filled by the papers of *A* and *B*, through the despair of the one and the resolve, self-knowledge and responsible activity of the other, points to something which is essentially incommunicable and indescribable, the *Either-Or* and the possibility of choice of oneself; he writes in the hope that someone among his readers will allow himself to be influenced by his Existential thinking towards what is more than a remembered possibility, to become attentive and active himself in response to the call. Just as in *Either-Or* Kierkegaard points to the possibility of a choice of oneself, so in the whole of his work he points to the possibility of becoming a Christian, for which choice of oneself is only the beginning.

8

Kierkegaard's Conception of " Existenz" and " Existential Thinking"

Turning from this example, we must ask, what does Existenz mean, and what is Existential thinking.

Existenz is not to be confused with Life. We remain in life from our birth to death. We find life in our fellow-men, in animals and in plants as well as within ourselves. We know bodily life with its health and sickness, its growth and ageing; mental life with its instincts, tensions and relaxations, conscious and unconscious; social life with its struggle for power in different organised forms; historical life with its civilisations that rise and fall[1].

It is not in this way that Existenz manifests itself. Man can originally experience its possibility only within himself. Yet it is not there from birth. It is not at all, but it becomes; or rather it may become. Existenz is an attitude of an individual towards himself, which is called forth by such concrete situations as the necessity for choice of profession or a conflict in love, a catastrophic change in social conditions, or the imminence of one's own death. It leads immediately to sublime moments in which man gathers his whole strength to make a decision which is taken afterwards

---

[1] Existenz, as can be seen from the following paragraph of the text, is also not to be confused with Existence in the usual sense of that term (in German "Dasein"). For while the term "Existence" can be used of many concrete things, such as matter, living beings or men, the term "Existenz", as employed by Kierkegaard, can be applied only to men and denotes even a special peculiarity of men, one example of which is brought forward by Kierkegaard's thoughts on "Choice" and some other characteristics of which are noted in the following paragraph. It may be worth mentioning that of the two principal philosophers who took up Kierkegaard's conception Jaspers strictly followed this distinction of "Existenz" not only from "Life", but also from "Existence", while Heidegger's use of the term "Existenz" is less strict and more akin to the general term "Human Existence", though from some of his analyses, such as that of the existential significance of death, and of conscience, one can grasp why he preferred the term "Existenz" to that of "Human Existence".

6-2

as binding upon his future life. Furthermore, Existenz never becomes completed, as does life through death. In its different manifestations it is only a beginning which is faithfully followed or faithlessly forgotten. Moreover, Existenz is not real in being known, it is real only when effectuated, in the remembrance of it, and in resolutions for the future which are taken to be absolutely binding.

So much for the conception of Existenz.

Existential thinking is, in the first place, an essential accompaniment of the realisation of Existenz. It can then call attention to the possibility of Existenz, as does Kierkegaard's moral man in *Either-Or*. Beyond all this, it represents, in its bearing, a type of thinking, which provides a new principle of reasoning in philosophy. This principle may be characterised thus:

(1) Philosophical thinking must start from the *actual life between birth and death*, in which we live; one must start neither from metaphysical speculations, for instance about the Divine, nor from a detached investigation of the forms of our understanding. In this respect Kierkegaard agrees with Nietzsche and Dilthey and their followers, and is opposed to Hegel as well as to the epistemologists.

(2) The deepest and most real things in life are experienced by the *individual in his inner decisions*, which depend on their own kind of clarifying thinking. By his insistence on the all-importance of these inner decisions, Kierkegaard's thought differs fundamentally from the "Philosophy of Life" in the sense of Dilthey, and it is distinguished to a certain extent from that of

Nietzsche, who does not attribute the same importance to the inner nature of the individual.

Such reflection on the inner life of the individual might seem unnecessary, when any authority reaching beyond human life is recognised, and if the autonomy of mind has not been called in question. But since real life is the only basis for thinking and philosophy, it is necessary for the thinker to become clear on the question where, in this life, he experiences reality at its deepest. And this is the more essential because, confronted with these deepest experiences, he finds himself again thrown back on the use of his own thinking and judgment. The philosophical importance of Kierkegaard, which distinguishes his thought from that of the mystics, lies in his conception of the relation between the realisation of Existenz and the special kind of knowledge involved in Existential thinking.

(3) This Existential thinking is, according to Kierkegaard, the *deepest kind of cognitive penetration into reality*. Thence arises the task of comparing such a form of knowledge with other kinds of knowledge and of establishing anew after such an examination the relative significance of the different special and previously connected kinds of knowledge and of correlating them. From this point of view Kierkegaard gained important insight into the relation of Existential thinking to the modes of thinking, adopted in psychology, involved in ethical demands, and in religious dogmas. Thus, he was also able to attack Hegel's speculative philosophy from a positive standpoint, and to criticise Kant's *Critique of Practical Reason*. For in

Hegel's philosophy the concrete actualities are considered only in the light of the general possibilities of thinking, the individual thinker diverting his attention from reality and its task, satisfying himself with speculations that are only intellectually all-embracing. Kant, on the other hand, is, according to Kierkegaard, right in pointing out in his *Critique of Pure Reason* the limitations of pure thought and of the generally accepted forms of understanding. But in his *Critique of Practical Reason*, by introducing the categorical imperative and his conception of freedom, he tries to prove more than his purely critical principle permits.

I can hardly hope in this brief account to have succeeded in making clear what Kierkegaard meant by Existenz and Existential thinking; this can be fully understood only from the study of his writings. Since, however, I have undertaken to indicate the trend of Contemporary German Philosophy, it seemed necessary to endeavour to convey at least a general impression of these conceptions.

For, together with Nietzsche's "Critique of Science", his "Conception of the Philosopher" and his "Philosophy of Life", and perhaps more than these, Kierkegaard's ideas of the "Existenz" of the individual and of Existential thinking have given rise to the deeper and more creative efforts of contemporary philosophical thought. They have led back to the universal tasks of philosophy, which cannot be attacked by any specialised branch of knowledge, and which in the philosophy of the nineteenth century, under the influence of autonomous science, had been neglected.

CHAPTER III

PRESENT DAY PHILOSOPHY

I

Brief survey of the continuance of academic tradition

Before I begin to describe Jaspers and Heidegger, the two German philosophers of to-day who more than any others have tried to understand the essence of philosophy and its future tasks, I want to emphasise that in Germany since the decade before the War many different tendencies have been noticeable in philosophical research, and that nothing would be a greater mistake than to take Jaspers and Heidegger as the only representatives of present German Philosophy.

I should like to go into these different tendencies in somewhat more detail, especially because, in the academic philosophy of the last thirty years, an unusually high standard has been reached in logical training, in the analysis of phenomena and problems and in research on the history of thought, of philosophy and of the separate sciences. The attainment of such a standard was favoured by the prosperous yet unsettled pre-War period in Germany; and, as a consequence of the War, this philosophical and scholarly culture has seriously declined among the younger generation, especially since 1925.

In view, however, of the plan of this work I must abstain from giving an account of the able research accomplished in the history of philosophy during these decades;[1] and from discussing the discoveries made in

[1] To such researchers belong, besides Cassirer, Misch, N. Hartmann and Spranger (other aspects of whose work will be discussed in the text), Karl Reinhardt (*Parmenides und die Geschichte der griechischen Philosophie*; *Poseidonios*; *Kosmos und Sympathie*; *Platon's Mythen*; *Poseidonios über Ursprung und Entartung*), Werner Jaeger (*Entstehungsgeschichte der Metaphysik des Aristoteles*; *Aristoteles, Grundlegung einer Geschichte seiner Entwicklung*; *Platos Stellung im Aufbau der griechischen Bildung*), Julius Stenzel (*Studien zur Entwicklung der platonischen Entwicklung von Sokrates bis zu Aristoteles*; *Zahl und Gestalt bei Aristoteles*; *Platon der Erzieher*; "Metaphysik des Altertums" in *Handbuch der Philosophie*, hrsg. v. Schroeter-Bäumler), Heinz Heimsoeth (*Die sechs Themen der abendländischen Metaphysik und der Ausgang des Mittelalters*; *Metaphysik der Neuzeit*), Richard Kroner (*Von Kant bis Hegel*, 2 Bände), Herman Schmalenbach (*Leibniz*; *Kants Religion*).

The historical investigations of the last decades have been especially concerned with the philosophy of two different periods, with that of Greece from its earliest beginnings down to Aristotle and with that of Germany from Nicholas of Cusa to Hegel. Especially noteworthy in this connection are, on the one hand, the interest shown since the time of Nietzsche in the pre-Socratic philosophers, and, on the other hand—apart from the renewed appreciation of the great philosophers of German Idealism, not only Fichte and Hegel, but also Schelling, especially in his later works—the rediscovery of Nicholas of Cusa (whose works are being edited by Hoffmann and Klibansky) and the deeper understanding of Leibniz' philosophy.

It should be remembered that, in Germany, the history of philosophy is increasingly regarded as an "Organon" of philo-

psychology and psychopathology.[1] Instead, I shall confine myself to mentioning a few especially prominent personalities and movements.

First, I must draw attention to two isolated figures: Nicolai Hartmann and Ernst Cassirer, both of them originally pupils of Ernst Cohen. Nicolai Hartmann has modelled his views under the influence of pheno-

sophy, and that therefore the researches in this field do not constitute a separate science in the ordinary sense of that term. Owing to the development of the historical consciousness through Herder, Hegel, the great historians of the early nineteenth century, Nietzsche and Dilthey, the conviction has been more and more gaining ground that present-day philosophy cannot be separated from the work of the great thinkers of the past, and that, only by entering into the spirit and the aims of the former thinkers, can we comprehend and fulfil our own tasks.

[1] Nevertheless, the development of psychology in Germany has been so important and its connection with philosophy so close, that the principal changes which it has brought about must be briefly outlined. These changes are chiefly due to two different groups of studies. The first, taking as its principal method the observation of behaviour, investigates the mentality of the abnormal (Freud, Adler, Bleuler, Jung, Jaspers, Kretschmer), of children (Groos, Stern, Koffka, K. and Ch. Bühler), of the higher animals (W. Köhler, Wasmann, Kafka, v. Frisch) and of primitive peoples; developing from these researches various, often dogmatic, theories of instincts. The second group (which Spranger called "geisteswissenschaftliche Psychologie") is concerned with personality, whether developed and creative in social and historical life or fulfilling inner or contemplative purposes; such investigations have been initiated by Kierkegaard, Nietzsche, Dilthey and Brentano, and among those who

menology, especially in its more realistic tendency as represented by Scheler, Geiger and Pfänder. He is concerned with an ontology of different spheres of reality (matter, life, soul, mind), in the sense that he treats of the problems, underlying the different sciences, in their individual character and their insolubility. Out of this conviction of the "insolubility" of philosophical problems arises the peculiar character of his "aporetic" ontology, towards which he has offered valuable contributions in three systematic books, *Metaphysics of Knowledge*; *Ethics*, and the recently published *Problem of the Objective Mind*.

Ernst Cassirer has two great merits. Firstly he is a leading authority on the history of science and of philosophy, as is clear from his *Geschichte des Erkenntnisproblems*, published before the War, as well as from his subsequent studies of the philosophy of the Renais-

have carried them further, Jaspers, Klages and Spranger are the foremost.

These more recent fruitful endeavours, whose object has been to observe and describe without preconceptions the dynamic forces and the richness of psychic phenomena, have put an end to the traditional psychology, which, after the model of the natural sciences, tried to construct the life of the soul out of separate elements, and in which a division of the soul, based on historical conceptions, into thought, will and feeling was for a long time prevalent. Moreover, this new psychology is in process of revising the traditional views of the connection between body and soul and of the identification, predominant since Descartes, of soul with consciousness. But it has not yet succeeded in attaining a unitary theory, based on universally acceptable principles.

sance, of the Age of Enlightenment and of the German Humanism of 1800. Secondly, Cassirer has the credit of having developed the ideas of Cohen's Neo-Kantianism and of having formulated the functional character of philosophy, in his book *Substanz-begriff und Funktions-begriff* (1910), as a task always to be pursued, though never to be completed. Starting from this, he has in his recent *Philosophie der symbolischen Formen* analysed the conceptual forms in myths, in language, and in scientific knowledge.

Of these men the first is pre-eminent for his thorough and penetrating analysis of problems and "aporiai", the second, for his comprehensive learning and the breadth of his culture, to which the productive character of his work is largely due.

I now pass to the two philosophical movements, which seem to me most important: that of the phenomenological school, founded by Husserl, and the movement led by Dilthey and his followers.

The significance of Husserl's school has already been touched upon in the first chapter. What was common to men like Pfänder, Geiger, Scheler, Reinach and Heidegger is, that they all have analysed and described the conceptual meanings of definite phenomena; these meanings being directly accessible to intuition, they can so to speak be "read off" straight from the phenomena without comprehensive philosophical constructions. The fact that in Germany during the last twenty years clarity, thoroughness and methodical training in the investigation of single phenomena have been considered a matter of course was due particularly to the various phenomenological schools that were inspired by the work of Husserl.

The Dilthey group, to which belong Misch, Nohl, Spranger, Groethuysen, Freyer, concentrated, as did Dilthey himself, on the study of the development of mind through the course of history. They analysed phenomena like that of autobiography in history; the dependence of artistic styles on the three types of Weltanschauung laid down by Dilthey; the variety of definite forms of life (for instance the aesthetic type of character, the theoretical, the political, the social, the economic, the religious); or the peculiarities of bourgeois views on life and the world; or the qualities of the objective mind. And though these researchers are inferior to the phenomenological investigations in the strictness and minuteness of their structural analyses, the work of the Dilthey school is enriched by an incomparably fuller comprehension of the actualities of the spiritual life in history. Furthermore, it was a special characteristic of men of this school such as Nohl and Spranger that they endeavoured to render their philosophical conceptions effective in public life. Carrying out Dilthey's principle, that philosophy should play an enlightening and educating rôle in public life, they became leading educationalists of the post-War period.

In contrast to these great movements, during the last twenty years two other philosophical schools sprang up which took the natural sciences as their basis. Wertheimer, Wolfgang Köhler, Koffka, Gelb and others created the "Gestalttheorie" which stresses the view that a method of scientific analysis is possible besides the usual one of analysing a phenomenon into its elements. They showed that the latter method may lead to the loss of features essential to scientific enquiry. In particular their principle, that the whole is more than its parts, has become very fruitful in psychology. The second school is that of the "scientific philosophy" of Schlick, Carnap and Reichenbach, which, in opposition to nearly all the other tendencies of to-day, narrows philosophy to scientific analysis, performed by the methods of symbolic logic, and to research mainly into the foundations of mathematical and physical knowledge.

If I refrain from going into more detail about these and other tendencies and in this last chapter confine myself to a review of the philosophy of Jaspers and Heidegger, I do so because I believe that the high level of philosophical scholarship, which is shown in the activity of these many trends of research, must not be allowed to distract us from the main issue, which is that German philosophy, in this era of autonomous sciences, has not emerged from the profound crisis into which it fell with the collapse of Hegel's philosophy. Therefore, the question: What are the essence and tasks of philosophy? remains of vital importance; and the answer given to this question will be decisive for the relevance of all future philosophy. Since this is so, and since, if I am not mistaken, the entire development of post-Hegelian philosophy has centred around this question, a grasp of which is essential to the understanding of the successive stages from Lotze, Fechner and Wundt to

Cohen, Windelband, Driesch and further to Husserl, Dilthey and Weber, I feel justified in devoting this chapter mainly to Jaspers and Heidegger. For under the influence of Nietzsche and Kierkegaard they have taken up this vital question and carried its elucidation one step further.

As another illustration of the difficult and uncertain situation of philosophy in our time it may be well to mention the fact, that both Jaspers and Heidegger took as their standard the great philosophy achieved before the crisis: Jaspers concentrating especially on Kant and Hegel, and Heidegger, on the Greek tradition from Parmenides to Aristotle. Yet it is apparent that their philosophising has deep roots in the present. Jaspers was originally trained in the natural sciences and in medicine, and at the beginning of his career made remarkable contributions to psychiatric and psychological research; further, he was strongly influenced by Kierkegaard, and also, to some extent, by Weber. Heidegger, originally of the Catholic world and possessing an intimate knowledge of such great medieval philosophers as Augustine, Aquinus and Duns Scotus, was trained by Husserl in phenomenological method; and at the same time, besides taking over certain of Kierkegaard's philosophical conceptions, hitherto unstudied, he adopted important ideas from Dilthey and Bergson, and also, increasingly of late, from Nietzsche. It may, I think, be said of both Jaspers and Heidegger that they succeeded further than other academic philosophers in finding a way back to that inner attitude and to those tasks which, through the rise of the autonomous sciences, had been lost to German philosophy since the era of Hegel; and that, at the same time, they endeavoured to maintain the critical strictness and the reflection on fundamental principles, which Kant had left as a model to the epistemologists of the later nineteenth century.

2

Jaspers' conception of the philosophical attitude; his three ways of philosophising

Karl Jaspers' philosophical work, taken generally, seems to me to be characterised by two features which are inherent in the man who stands behind it: a deep earnestness from which he derives a feeling of absolute responsibility for his actions and even his knowledge, and a boundless desire for clarity. His earnestness stimulates the will to clarity so that he cannot be satisfied with research into detail, but proceeds more and more towards the comprehensive and fundamental, from the single fact to the whole of a science, to a universal consideration, finally to philosophy itself. Owing to this will to clarity, his earnestness not only manifests itself in immediate practical activity, but becomes philosophically productive in critical analysis.

Already in his first book, *Allgemeine Psychopathologie*, which immediately after its appearance in 1913 became the standard work on this science, the logical clarity with which Jaspers distinguishes the different methods employed in the subject is very remarkable. This is seen in his distinctions between the consideration of subjective phenomena, the objective study of effects, the psychology of expression, the understanding of connections, the causal explanation of connections, the formation of theories, the conception of totalities like intelligence or personality, the conception of totality which is commonly described as a disease and the sociological relations of abnormal mental life. "We must learn to know what we know, and what we do not know; how, and in what sense, and within what limits, we know anything; by what means this knowledge has been obtained, and upon what it is founded."[1] With these words Jaspers formulates his intense will to clarity in his first work.

His second important work was the *Psychologie der Weltanschauungen*, which appeared in 1919. Here one can feel the tension between his driving earnestness and his determination to maintain the attitude of a detached onlooker. Inspired by Nietzsche's and Kierkegaard's psychology, but aiming at a strictly scientific method, he analyses the possible attitudes of man towards the world, and finally, as the fundamental determining factor, the decisions which the individual man must make in inescapable situations (Grenzsituationen), such as those due to the inevitability of death, struggle, chance, guilt. He proceeds to the analysis of the various possible ways in which man meets these situations, either dissolution in scepticism and Nihilism, or taking refuge in fixed conventions, or the support found in Existential thinking and in the realisation of "Existenz".

Twelve years later, in 1931, Jaspers published a

[1] *Allgemeine Psychopathologie*, S. VII, Vorwort zur 3. Auflage.

three-volume work, entitled *Philosophie*, in which he endeavours to set forth his philosophical views upon the totality of experience. Since he is convinced that in philosophy, unlike science, there can be no essential progress he insists that the crucial task of every philosopher must be to objectivate this totality for himself in a new and fundamental way. Jaspers' work, in that it is presented in a complete form, stands in contrast to that of Nietzsche and Kierkegaard which, although the chief source of inspiration to contemporary German philosophers, did not go far towards giving a systematic explanation of their own philosophical thoughts, to that of Husserl and Dilthey who were responsible for our present method of analysis and for our philosophical interpretation of history but did not progress beyond a fragmentary formulation, and to that of Heidegger whose writings so far have only partially expressed his philosophical aims.

Particularly important and deserving of further study appears to me his *methodological conception* that *in all philosophising* from the earliest times to the present *three fundamentally different methods* have existed. Originally undistinguished, becoming more clearly separated in the course of time, but never until now entirely differentiated, these three methods working together have constituted all that can, or ever could, claim the title of philosophy. They are:

(1) The philosophical world-orientation (Philosophische Weltorientierung).

(2) The elucidation of Existenz (Existenzerhellung).

(3) The way of metaphysics (Metaphysik).

Now, what constitutes the first kind of philosophising? To explain this I must begin farther back.

The researches of the scientist give us insight into the inter-relation of separate phenomena in the world. The importance and special achievements of the separate sciences (which, for example, Nietzsche has questioned and the limits and significance of which Weber has sought to define), Jaspers finds in that special kind of thinking which by self-discipline searches for objectivity, and which establishes new knowledge which is admitted by fellow-workers in the science to be certain and objectively true. In this way the scientists gain a limited and relative insight into single groups of phenomena in the world, but they orientate themselves to these phenomena only in so far as scientific enquiry is never finished but is a continuing process. In this respect, all the sciences together constitute an *enquiring world-orientation* (forschende Welt-orientierung).

Subsequently one may attempt to *complete artificially* such scientific knowledge, and this has been attempted in two ways by *Positivism* and by *Idealism*. The former tries to construct a picture of the world by identifying objective Being with Being in general; or else, by mistaking Being for that special sort of Being which is cognisable in space and time by the methods of the natural sciences. The latter takes Being to be identical either with the subject conscious of himself, or the idea which is apprehended dialectically as the synthesis of subject and object. Thus Positivism thinks it has made reality accessible. Idealism thinks it has made truth accessible, in an absolute sense. But both transcend the variety of phenomena which is actually available and cognisable by science in its objective search.

Against these false attempts to make genuine knowledge absolute the *philosophical world-orientation* (philosophische Weltorientierung) is directed, and in pointing out the necessity that scientific enquiry should be conscious of its *incompleteness*, the philosopher with his world-orientation recognises that his own knowledge of the phenomena in the world must remain equally incomplete. It is the particular object of the first chapters of Jaspers' book to bring home the necessary incompleteness of our world-orientation by analysing our conception of the world, the limits of the world-orientation and the systematic presentation of the sciences. Thus, for example, he points out that neither the existence of the subject, nor the objective reality in itself, can lead to a unitary knowledge of the world. On the other hand, he analyses the antinomies involved in our thinking of the world, as given or as made, as a universe or as a mere world-interpretation, as the reality in itself or as the manifestation of one being. So he expounds the limits of our world-orientation, by first showing that in scientific research a compelling proof is indispensable, either in the form of compelling thought in mathematics and logic, or of compelling reality in the empirical objectivity of Natural and Humanistic Sciences, or of compelling intuition in the essentials and categories of objective Beings. He then proceeds to point out the relativity of all compelling demonstration in these three fields. He explains as another limit of the world-orientation the insurmountable end-lessness in subjective methods and objective reality of research, expressed by Kant's concepts of "Idea" and "Antinomy". So he points out, in a systematic ex-position of the sciences, the impossibility of the for-mation of a universally valid system of knowledge by showing the contradictory character of the possible principles for the order of such a system. So finally he emphasises the character of reality as fundamentally split up into matter, life, soul, mind, between which there are unbridged gaps; and he shows the inadequacy of either denying or making absolute or reducing these various realities.

These few examples will be enough to show how Jaspers, not only in a special science like psychopatho-logy, but in the whole of enquiring world-orientation, tries to separate what we know and what we do not know and to describe contradictions, limits, incompre-hensibilities.

But why does he do this? Is it only to call attention to all these contradictions, limits, incomprehensibilities? In what lies the essential of such a method of philo-sophising?

Jaspers answers: The knowledge obtained by scientific enquiry is always in danger of becoming fixed and rigid and has to be called into question by philosophy. It must be shown as what it actually is, and one must not be allowed to be satisfied with an illusion of perfection that cannot by its nature belong to knowledge obtained by scientific enquiry. Such attempts to call knowledge in question have in fact always been made by real philosophers, the most note-worthy being that of Kant in his *Critique of Pure Reason*, but this tendency is often to be traced, especially in periods in which knowledge is highly developed. And this is so because it is the function of the first method of philosophising to point out the limits of rational knowledge, and thereby to save philosophy from illusory satisfaction in its search after the essential.

A second way of philosophising, essentially different from the first, originates in the conduct of human life; namely in that conduct of human life which, unsatisfied by daily existence with its variety of changing situations and of actions which have only limited aims, strives to satisfy the deepest demands of human nature, thus trying to realise Existenz in the sense of Kierkegaard. To realise Existenz in life is obviously, as already shown with regard to Kierkegaard's conception of choice, not a demand which dominates the life of everyone; if it were, Plato's State, where philosophers were kings, would not be merely Utopia. But every genuine philo-sopher as an individual has probably at least once in his life experienced the demand for the realisation of Existenz, and all his philosophising can, from one view-point, only be understood as an elucidation of such a demand. And since no one lives entirely indepen-dently of society, it is also the desire of the philosopher, who is conscious that such a demand is serious and inescapable, to appeal to other individuals and to re-mind them of the demands which they themselves may have experienced. It is, of course, the indubitable right of every individual either to resist or to respond to such appeals. There is no authority above the individual, neither Understanding nor Reason, which can decide, advise or command upon the question of these absolute inner demands for the conduct of life. On the contrary, the individual himself must, freely, and on his own absolute responsibility, choose and decide his conduct of life. To direct the attention of the individual to such a possible freedom, and to awaken his sense of absolute responsibility is the second way of philosophising called by Jaspers *Elucidation of Existenz* (Existenzerhellung).

Since, within the limits of this essay, the deep and thorough analyses which Jaspers endeavoured to give as such an Elucidation cannot be described in detail, I shall bring forward only the following points. As a first presupposition of the realisation of Existenz, he describes, starting from Kierkegaard's distinction between Existenz and Life, the apprehension of the "I-myself", placing it in contrast to the thinking consciousness in general and to the vital and social forces in life. As another such presupposition, he describes the relationship of free individuals which he calls "communication", this being the process by which they become more and more comprehensible and real to one another. Analysing this communication in more detail he describes the defects which may occur, such as the experience that communication may remain vague or fail or that there may be a lack of response or lack of respect, or the further possibility that the communication may break down through fear or because of egoistic resistance, etc. He further analyses the process of the realisation of Existenz in the single self in communication with other selves by considering the historical structure of the individual life, which reveals itself for instance in the fidelity or infidelity of the individual to other individuals or to his decisions or to his faith.

These three together, the "I-myself", "communication" and "historical structure", form the basis for any realisation or elucidation of Existenz, just as the conception of the World is the basis for common-sense knowledge in general.

The basic analysis of these phenomena is followed by a still deeper exposition of Existenz under the title "being-oneself as freedom"; and by a further thorough explanation of the forces by which the individual actually realises Existenz, when he, in view of the inescapability of Grenzsituationen such as Death, Suffering, Struggle and Guilt, is led by an absolute consciousness of Love, Faith and Imagination; and when he therefore acts unconditionally, either transcending his own existence, as in a religious act, or in suicide, or by realising himself in inner action or action in the world.

I have mentioned these few points only because I believe that the investigations I have enumerated form the most creative contributions of Jaspers' entire work. But for us here the important thing is to understand that this second method of *appealing to freedom* and of *ascertaining Existenz* is to be separated essentially from the first method of *calling in question fixed knowledge*. The first method has the negative purpose of showing the essential incomprehensibility of the things in the world to our rational consciousness. In the second method the philosopher addresses himself positively to others on the subject of their freedom, as has been done by Plato, the Stoics, Spinoza, Kant, Fichte, and many others, and has been recognised as a specific kind of thinking first by Kierkegaard.

But such a recognition of freedom, as has been said above, cannot be supported by conceptions like reason or mind. On the contrary, the characteristic of such conceptions lies in their being themselves synthetic products of different methods; Kant's conception of reason, for instance, must be understood as a synthetic product of his intention to call in question fixed knowledge and to express the imperative demands of his inner nature. What is essential in philosophising is not such "organs" as reason or mind, but the *search for the truth*, according to the different methods. And the methods of calling in question fixed knowledge and of appealing to freedom are as different from one another as, for example, the intuitive understanding of a state of mind, due to observing a certain facial expression, is different from a causal explanation of such a facial expression as a symptom of a mental disease.

Jaspers' third way of philosophising is the *way of metaphysics*. It originates because an individual in his search for truth cannot be satisfied with knowledge of a variety of objective things, nor with the realisation of his own Existenz or that of others. Moreover, it is precisely in his supreme moments that the individual realises most certainly that, though he may be able to

"choose himself" and to "accept himself", to desire
the good, and to act with determination, he has not
created himself, nor will he ever be able entirely to
remodel himself as he sometimes might wish to do.
From such an experience of his own limitations, from
the bonds that unite him to other individuals, and from
questions such as "Why is there being and not
nothing?" (which was asked by Leibniz and Schelling),
there arises a consciousness of being *relative* to something other than oneself, to something absolute, *to one
being* (das eine Sein). But the philosopher cannot be
certain of the "one being" in the same sense that the
religious man is certain of God, nor in the sense that
we are certain of objective things. The experience of the
"one being" is also different from the experience of
inner commands to realise Existenz of which the individual becomes aware in his thought and actions.
It arises only as an ultimate possibility in the seeking of
those who try to realise Existenz in spite of its fragmentary character. It reveals itself in the *contemplative
play of the imagination* of the individual, which is
the origin of Jaspers' third method of philosophising,
the method of metaphysics. Although, according to
Jaspers the "one being" cannot be enunciated with absolute certainty as prophetic philosophy down to Hegel
claimed to do, and although it cannot be approached
by the way of scientific enquiry, such as has been tried
in the nineteenth century and is even attempted to-day,
nevertheless, in the course of philosophy there has
grown up a language in which, for many centuries,
metaphysicians have expressed their thought. This lan-

guage of metaphysics was in the nineteenth century no longer understood; its significance must now be rediscovered by an analysis of its peculiar forms of thought.

Within metaphysics itself Jaspers distinguishes *three different methods* reflecting the three different methods of philosophising.

The first is *formal transcending*, the elevation of thought from the determinate object to the indeterminable, such as is found in dialectics (e.g. in Plato's *Parmenides*, in Nicholas of Cusa, and in Hegel) in a synthesis of contradictory thoughts, such as of being and not being, of unity and duality, etc. Here, by using the tool of objective knowledge and making positive use of the contradictory character of reality, room is made, formally, for the possibility of the "one being".

In another way, from the *realisation of Existenz* arises a positive seeking for the "one being", in so far as we find ourselves subjected to *ultimately irreconcilable tendencies*, such as defiance and devotion, elevation and fall, obedience to law and order and the instinct to revolt, delight in the manifold values of the world and consciousness of the "one being".

The third way is the "*Reading of the cyphers of the one-being*", as Jaspers, following German Humanism of 1800, calls it. Such a cypher has many different meanings, and is not to be taken in a definite sense. In the course of history the "one being" has been conceived by different individuals, to be nature, history, consciousness in general, mankind. The "one being", concealed in such a cypher, has been expressed in great art and has been interpreted in speculative philosophy.

By these different methods, metaphysical symbols of the past can be *assimilated* anew, in a methodologically clear manner. But this is only possible, when the presupposition that one attempts to realise the absolute inner demands and the freedom of one's own life is fulfilled. For only he who is clear about the contradictions and the split-up character of reality, and who undeterred follows the absolute inner demands of his nature, will be conscious of being relative to the "one being" in the contemplative play of metaphysics.

So much for the three methods of philosophising as distinguished in principle by Jaspers, who regards them as constituting the ways of all philosophising of the past and present.

For us, however, in our consideration of contemporary philosophy, Jaspers seems important in that, living with us in the age of highly developed science, and himself a very productive investigator in psychopathology and psychology, he has explained in a new and modern sense the meaning of philosophy in contrast to science.

For him the task of philosophy does not lie in a synthesis of the knowledge obtained by the special sciences, as it did for Fechner, Lotze, Eduard v. Hartmann and Wundt. On the contrary, for him one task of philosophy is to exclude the artificial and pictorial constructions of totality which Positivism and Idealism both attempt, from the ever open world-orientation of research. Nor does he, like Cohen, Windelband and

Rickert, limit philosophy to an understanding of the principles of science, however much he himself investigates the peculiar character of objective research with its often conflicting tendencies to investigate minutely and to grasp the really essential features. Nor is he satisfied in carrying out an analysis of meaning in the phenomenological sense of the term, although he appreciates that here there is a philosophical method distinct from science. Nor would he be content with Dilthey's reflections on the relation of the various Weltanschauungen to the historical life.

For philosophy is to Jaspers the never satisfied search for truth in the world of knowledge, in the conduct of life, and in the seeking for the "one being" as this is dimly seen through our antithetic thoughts, deep existential conflicts and multifarious cyphers. Philosophy to-day as in ancient Greece always originates from the individual man who, bounded by the narrow limits of this short life, is bold enough to enter upon an intellectual struggle with totality, out of a last incomprehensible impulse seeking truth about this existence, in which we find ourselves, and trying to gain as far as possible a clear and distinct consciousness of it. That philosophy has a responsible and unique task today, to-morrow and for ever, as great now as before the autonomous development of the sciences which, without touching it or its essential tasks, has only helped to increase its desire for clarity; this Jaspers has emphasised as no one else of his contemporaries.

Heidegger's conception of a new philosophical theme; the analysis of human existence as a preparatory explanation for the problem of being

While Jaspers by his presentation of the three ways of philosophising tries to awaken the desire for a fuller and more genuine philosophy, Martin Heidegger seeks to perform the same task, though in an entirely different way. He has never been a psychologist or methodologist like Jaspers, and he has been little concerned with the methods of philosophising. But what is constantly before him is that which he regards as the true theme of philosophy—the one question, which inspired all Greek thinkers from Parmenides to Aristotle, and which has continuously determined the course of Christian and modern philosophy—the search for the meaning of Being. This problem of Being which to-day has become for us so obvious that we no longer reflect upon its meaning, so obvious indeed that it is even forgotten, Heidegger endeavours to raise again, but in a way entirely different from that of the Greek philosophers.

Being and Time is the title of the work in which Heidegger, by a phenomenological analysis of human existence, especially in respect of its temporal and historical character, endeavours to open a new approach to the philosophical problem of Being. This approach has been rendered possible for him by Kant's transcendental philosophy, by the Christian experience of thinkers like Augustine and Kierkegaard, by the historical consciousness which Herder aroused in Germany, which Dilthey thought out and which Nietzsche recognised in its significance for human life, and finally by Husserl's deliberate phenomenological method; nevertheless, it is due to his own energy of thought which has never slackened in the thorough working-out of his ideas, and to his practised conceptual and linguistic art, that one continuous trend of thought has become apparent, as is nowhere else the case in contemporary German philosophy. The significance of this title, *Being and Time*, and Heidegger's aim in the philosophical investigations begun under this title, I shall now try to explain briefly.

If we wish to go beyond the type of phenomenological analysis which is merely Heidegger's craft to what is essential in his thought, we must first consider his peculiar relation to the history of philosophy and to history in general. For Heidegger who, as already indicated, began his career as a philosopher in an inner discussion with the Catholic religion and its highest intellectual expression, medieval philosophy, concentrated with unusual intensity and thoroughness on the philosophising of the great thinkers of the past; thus he approached it, not in the calm and self-satisfied manner of the post-Hegelians of the nineteenth century, who regarded the history of philosophy as a set of important, though antiquated and unrealisable, doctrines, but rather in the way in which an independent and thoughtful, though devout, Christian might read the Bible. Just as such a Christian may find, besides much that is of little account to him, certain truths so deep and valid that they, far from being antiquated because they were first proclaimed millenniums ago, make most of what is said to-day appear feeble and superficial and give to the believer strength for his whole life and work, so Heidegger's thinking, inspired by an ever more urgent desire to penetrate to the first origins, has matured by a continuous study of great philosophers, of Descartes, Leibniz, Kant, Fichte, Schelling, Hegel; of Augustine, Aquinus, Kierkegaard; and finally and above all of Aristotle, Plato and the thinkers before Socrates.

One important result of this unusual study of the history of philosophy was that to Heidegger the ambiguity in the tradition which forms our life became increasingly apparent. Tradition, whether in philosophy or in religion or in the life of a nation, arising from the inner relation of men to their historical past, no doubt seems to remind them of the important facts of the past, and to awaken in them historical consciousness. But how seldom does this really happen! How seldom does one succeed in penetrating through the hardened tradition to the underlying facts that are really worthy of remembrance! Tradition as such, according to Heidegger, especially when it is dominant, ordinarily conceals from us the real course and meaning of former events; it deprives the individual of the power of guiding himself, of questioning and choosing for himself, and by making what has been handed down appear natural, it allays his doubts and prevents him from determinedly going back to the already obscured sources.

It is Heidegger's conviction that, at least in philosophy, the greatest and most influential thoughts have already been brought forth, but that we in our present consciousness, which with regard to philosophy goes so little to the real origins, have forgotten the truths that were discovered, with the result that we, far from having advanced beyond the great thinkers of the past, have lost the ability to take at all seriously that philosophising which once has been realised. And so Heidegger requires, and himself tries to accomplish, a destruction of what has come down to us in the history of philosophy, not in order to free himself from the past, but in order, by avoiding the hardened dogmas and secondary problems, to find his way back to the original philosophical experiences from which the first and hence leading conceptions of philosophy have been created. It is his hope and aim, by this re-discovery of the hidden sources, to revive the genuine philosophising which, in spite of appearances to the contrary, has almost vanished from the life of to-day.

By thus immersing himself in the history of philosophy, Heidegger comes to recognise that Greek thinkers from Anaximander, Parmenides and Heraclitus to Plato and Aristotle philosophised in an incomparably fuller sense, that is, searched more radically for the ultimate reasons and first principles, than has since been done. The problem of Being, formulated for the first time in Western history by the pre-Socratic philosophers, especially Parmenides, has, Heidegger thinks, inspired the enquiries of Plato and Aristotle, but thenceforth has sunk into the background as an explicit problem for actual philosophical research. What these two men, Plato and Aristotle, continuing the former investigations, had gained, has remained in spite of considerable deviations down to the "Logic" of Hegel. What once had been wrested from the phenomena by the highest, though incomplete, efforts of thought, has long since been made trivial, and moreover erected into a dogma which not only treats the quest for the meaning of Being as superfluous, but even justifies the absence of such a problem.

How Heidegger has further explained his unusual view, that philosophising in its deepest sense has not, since the time of the Greeks, come again into motion, being first hindered in free enquiry by the Christian dogma of revelation and then artificially narrowed by the predominance of mathematics, physics, and the analysis of consciousness since Descartes, I cannot here describe in more detail. I wish only to emphasise the fact that Heidegger assigns a unique importance, comparable to that of Plato and Aristotle, to Kant who, although in his questioning for Being dependent on the dogmatic tradition, in the transcendental turn of his philosophy was the first modern thinker to grasp again the original task of metaphysics and to carry it one stage beyond what had been discovered by the Greeks.

Nevertheless, beside the model of Greek philosophising with its restless and undogmatic questioning and searching after the meaning of Being, Heidegger recognises one essential limitation in the Greeks: that to them the pre-eminent example for Being was the individual existent thing in its visibility and perceptibility. When Aristotle develops his categories of substance, quantity, quality, relation, place, date, position, state, action and passivity, it is the individual existent and perceptible thing in which he distinguished such separate describable aspects; and the importance of seeing in Greek philosophy in general is likewise apparent from the origin and predominance of such conceptions as phenomenon, derived from φῶς, light, that which appears, shows itself in the light; and ἰδέα or εἶδος, that which can be seen. And from such perceptible existent things as the model kind of being, Greek philosophy interprets also life and even man as well as Being in itself, the world as the way of connection of all beings, and time as the presence of an individual existing thing.

In what way can such rigid limitations be overcome? Where are we to find new and more fundamental phenomena which open a new approach to the problem of Being than in the individual visible thing? That was Heidegger's question.

The answer, however, was prepared by some individual thinkers since the Greeks.

Augustine in his *Confessiones* philosophically reflected upon the ceaseless unrest which accompanies the individual in the perplexity of the course of his temporal life, with his memories, sense of guilt, resolutions, and hope—all different properties of the time-character of human existence; and such ceaseless unrest seems a more genuine basis for truth than the certainty of the classical philosophers with their confidence in the power of θεωρία.

Descartes in all his doubts was indubitably certain of the fact that he himself existed in his thinking, doubting and even in his being deceived, so long as he was consciously realising these processes.

Kant tried to sum up the three great questions of philosophy, "what can I know?" "what ought I to do?" "what may I hope?" in one fundamental question, "what is man?"

Dilthey recognised that the great task before us, to explain our modern philosophical consciousness of Being, was fundamentally different from that of the Greeks: the ancients interpreted life from their conception of the world; we must interpret the world from our conception of life, that is, of human life.[1]

And Kierkegaard realised that Hegel's speculation had fallen into error because he did not sufficiently regard the basic realities of human existence.

Starting from all such experiences and preparatory attempts, Heidegger attacks the problem of Being in a new way, namely by the preliminary question "what is man?" Just as the Greeks analysed the perceptible existent thing in its categorical structure in order to proceed to the question of Being, Heidegger tries with the same strictness of thought to analyse the much more intricate, but far more fundamental, problem of the structure of human existence. And it should be observed that his analysis is directed towards one essential feature of human existence which had not been deeply enough investigated by Greek philosophy and by the ontology dominated thereby down to Hegel—its temporal and

[1] Cf. *Gesammelte Schriften*, Bd. VII, S. 291.

historical character; this character of human existence seems to him of especial importance, as it seemed before to Dilthey, because it forms the horizon of all human questioning about Being, that is, of all philosophical thought.

From this explanation of what is really meant by the title *Being and Time* it is obvious that many hitherto unexplored phenomena are dealt with. It is noteworthy how Heidegger in his analyses of the phenomena of the world describes the relation of man to the perceptible thing taken for granted by the Greeks; how he discusses the fundamental constitution of the existence of man, as occupied with various concerns in the world, in his relations to his environment, to his fellow-men, and to himself; how he analyses this existing in the world with its characteristics of being placed in a certain situation, of understanding the situation and, through speech, of being able to interpret it; and how he characterises the relations of human existence to reality and truth. And only when these elementary analyses have been grasped, can one appreciate his further expositions of more complicated structures, such as the existential significance of death which the individual can anticipate in his mind, and so conceive of himself as a finite totality, and thereby attain conscience and the power of resolution; and as a consequence of this analysis he explains the phenomena of man's position in daily life and history, thus approaching his ultimate problem of "Being and Time".

Heidegger's purpose in *Being and Time* is not, however, limited to directing attention to such unexplored phenomena but is to show that, far from having reached the end of philosophical enquiry, either in the sense of Hegel or of the scientists of the nineteenth century, we have hardly come in sight of the most fundamental problems which must be attacked, and that these problems must be attacked, not by science, which concerns itself with limited spheres of existence, but only by the philosophers of the future. Thus, by bringing forward a new thematic task for philosophy, his work complements that of Jaspers, who explains the significance of philosophising in its fullest sense. With this thematic task, which in its universality transcends all other endeavours of contemporary academic philosophy, Heidegger attempts to raise philosophy again to a height which in the nineteenth century, the age of science, it seemed to have lost for ever.

CONCLUSION

The still undecided position of Philosophy among the determining factors in human life

In the foregoing studies an attempt has been made to outline the gradual development of German philosophy since the time of Hegel. I was led to do this not only by the desire to introduce to my readers the work of some men which has not hitherto been described, but also by the hope that what has been accomplished during nearly a whole century in the realm of German thought, and the effects of which have until now been felt mainly in that country, may also be of some value outside Germany. And indeed the point of view from which this development of German philosophy seems to be especially worthy of attention is the sense of uncertainty prevalent to-day, as to the significance of philosophy for the lives of men. Accordingly, I propose to end this account with a brief survey of the forces which must be expected to determine human life in the future.

Some of these forces are already apparent:

(1) The importance of *technique*, which enables us to satisfy our physical wants and by which men are brought into closer external contact than ever before.

(2) The importance of *economic processes*, by which men try to gain the means of supplying their needs, and which, still more than technique, link men together within a nation and within the world.

(3) The importance of the single *State* internally and externally: internally as the unit in which power over numberless human beings is concentrated, and in which men struggle in manifold groups and organisations for their share of power and for the preservation or alteration of their government; externally as the unit which, in alliance with, or in opposition to, other States, makes effective its concentrated power in a manner which cannot be foreseen or directed by any individual.

(4) The importance of those *peoples outside of Europe* who, whether they have been formerly subjugated or awakened by Western culture and civilisation, have been trying since the middle of the nineteenth century and increasingly since the War to make their political power and their own civilisation effective, independently of, and possibly against, Europe.

Besides all these basic realities, there remains the undoubted importance of *science*, which investigates reality in its factual connections, and which is bound to be pursued, especially in the physical and biological-medical sciences, if only for practical reasons.

While all these factors—improbable contingencies aside—will continue as part of the life of Western man, the fate of *Christianity* is yet uncertain. No doubt, to-day as centuries ago, the Church provides many men with an interpretation of existence and thereby with spiritual strength for life—an apparently indispensable support for the masses, whose actual life is ruthlessly formed as well as left without purpose or inspiration by technique, economic life and the State. On the other hand, all these forces as well as the sciences act independently of and often in opposition to Christianity inasmuch as they seek to bind man to their particular aims and to develop ways of thinking suitable to these mundane purposes. Likewise philosophy, by its unlimited search for truth and its will to freedom, stands opposed at least to Christian dogma and to the principle of the authority of divine revelation, inherent in it.

Equally uncertain is the future significance of *Philosophy*. What will be its fate? In earlier modern times, although realised only by individuals like Descartes, Leibniz and Kant, Bruno and Spinoza, Bacon, Locke and Hume, philosophy lent intellectual justification to the whole life of an era. Will it do the same in the future? Will it accomplish the task, attempted for instance by Jaspers, of giving to an individual resolved upon freedom a philosophical consciousness, which would enable him to conduct himself more intelligently and decisively than the unphilosophical man? And will, as Heidegger for instance hopes, philosophy, starting from the knowledge of the structure of human existence, succeed in confronting us once more with the problem of Being? In short, will it be the task of future philosophy to interpret existence in a more universal sense and so once more give strength and significance to human life, as it did in Greece and in earlier modern times? Or will it manifest itself in a humbler, though certainly not unimportant manner, through the minute investigation of specialised problems propounded by isolated schools? That is the question which, in the future, must be decided for philosophy.

BIBLIOGRAPHY

The purpose of the following list of works is not to give a complete survey of the post-Hegelian philosophical literature of Germany. Those who wish for such survey will find it in the thorough volume IV, pp. 197–724, of Ueberweg, *Grundriss der Geschichte der Philosophie* (12. Aufl., völlig neubearbeitet von T. K. Oesterreich). Here I endeavour to mention mainly the works of scholars with whom the foregoing study have been concerned.

I have divided the list into two parts. In the first of these I deal with the leading thinkers who have been discussed at length in the text, and give, besides a list of their writings, some explanatory remarks with regard to their contents. The second part is little more than a list, in which I endeavour to show the most important works produced by the various schools of thought and by outstanding individuals.

PART 1

Works of the Principal Philosophers discussed

1. EDMUND HUSSERL, born 1859 in Prossnitz (Mähren), Emeritus Professor of Philosophy at Freiburg im Breisgau.

WORKS

Philosophie der Arithmetik, Halle, 1891.
Logische Untersuchungen, 2 Bände, Halle, 1900 ff.; zweite umgearbeitete Auflage, Bd. I und II 1, Halle, 1913, Bd. II 2, Halle, 1921.

CONTEMPORARY GERMAN PHILOSOPHY

"Philosophie als strenge Wissenschaft", in *Logos*, Bd. I, 1910 f.

Ideen ʒu einer reinen Phänomenologie und phänomenologischen Philosophie, I. Buch: "Allgemeine Einführung in die reine Phänomenologie", Halle, 1913 (first published in *Jahrbuch für Philosophie und phänomenologische Forschung*, Bd. I).

English translation: *Ideas: General Introduction to Pure Phenomenology*, translated by W. R. Boyce Gibson, London, Allen and Unwin, 1931.

"Vorlesungen zur Phänomenologie des inneren Zeitbewusstseins", Halle, 1928 (published in *Jahrb. f. Philos. u. phänomen. Forsch.*, Bd. IX).

"Formale und transzendentale Logik", Halle, 1929 (published in *Jahrb. f. Philos. u. phänomen. Forsch.*, Bd. X).

"Méditations Cartésiennes", Paris, Librairie Armand Colin, 1931 (published in *Bibliothèque de la Société Française de Philosophie*).

Especially important for the study of Husserl are: *Logische Untersuchungen, Ideen ʒu einer reinen Phänomenologie* and the article "Philosophie als strenge Wissenschaft". Only the six essays in the second volume of the *Logische Untersuchungen* are to be taken as essentially phenomenological investigations which should be read consecutively. The first essay in this volume on "Bedeutung und Ausdruck" will serve as a helpful introduction and essays 5 and 6, "Über intentionale Erlebnisse und ihre 'Inhalte'" and "Elemente einer phänomenologischen Aufklärung der Erkenntnis", are of especial importance. Besides these actual investigations, the exposition of the phenomenological method, given in the *Ideen*, should also be read. In contrast to these two fundamental works, *Logische Untersuchungen*, vol. I, offers only the programmatic enunciation of the autonomy of pure logic; and the article "Philosophie als strenge Wissenschaft" seeks to establish the strictly scientific, critical and analytic character of phenomenology in opposition to the then rising interest in Weltanschauung and Philosophy of Life. (Cf. *Weltanschauung*, Berlin, 1910, to which Dilthey, Simmel, Misch and other leading representatives of this tendency contributed.)

Here I wish at least to mention the great work of FRANZ BRENTANO (1838–1917), who, apart from his school represented by A. Marty, O. Kraus, A. Kastil, exercised a deep influence on Husserl, Meinong and Stumpf, so that it may be said that the development, at any rate, of logic in modern Germany is to a considerable extent indirectly due to him. Nevertheless, I thought it advisable to omit him from the account given in this book, because his writings, considered apart from his direct teaching, have so far had no important influence on Contemporary German Philosophy, whereas Husserl's *Logische Untersuchungen* and his elaboration of the phenomenological method have opened the way for philosophical systematic analysis. Brentano's collected philosophical works, 10 volumes, are being edited by O. Kraus and A. Kastil and have been in course of publication since 1922 in the Philosophische Bibliothek, Meiner, Leipzig.

2. WILHELM DILTHEY, 1833–1911, born in Biebrich a. Rhein, from 1882 Professor of Philosophy in Berlin.

WORKS

Gesammelte Schriften, Bd. I–IX, hrsg. von Misch, Nohl, Groethuysen und anderen, Leipzig-Berlin, 1913–34. (Vol. I contains his "Einleitung in die Geisteswissenschaften", vols. II–IV his historical studies concerning the modern

Weltanschauung from the sixteenth to the nineteenth
century, vols. v–viii his essentially systematic researches,
vol. ix his lectures on education.)

Das Leben Schleiermachers, Bd. 1, 2. verm. Aufl. hrsg. von H.
Mulert, Berlin, 1922.

Das Erlebnis und die Dichtung, 6. Aufl. Leipzig-Berlin, 1919
(containing essays on Lessing, Goethe, Novalis and Hölderlin).

Von deutscher Dichtung und Musik, hrsg. von Nohl und Misch,
Leipzig-Berlin, 1933.

Der junge Dilthey, ein Lebensbild in Briefen und Tagebüchern,
1852–70, zusammengestellt von Clara Misch geb. Dilthey,
Leipzig-Berlin, 1933.

Probably the most suitable introduction to Dilthey's
philosophy is "Das Wesen der Philosophie" (*Ges. Schr.*
Bd. v, S. 339 ff.). For a deeper study, besides the fundamental "Einleitung in die Geisteswissenschaften", volume
vii, centred around the "Aufbau der geschichtlichen Welt
in den Geisteswissenschaften" (S. 79 ff.), and volume viii,
centred around "Die Typen der Weltanschauung und ihre
Ausbildung in den metaphysischen Systemen" (S. 75 ff.),
are especially important. For the development of the newer
psychology was the essay "Ideen über eine beschreibende
und zergliedernde Psychologie" (Bd. v, S. 139 ff.) influential. In the field of Geistesgeschichte his "Weltanschauung und Analyse des Menschen seit Renaissance und
Reformation" (*Ges. Schr.* Bd. ii), "Jugendgeschichte
Hegels" (*Ges. Schr.* Bd. iv, S. 5–180), *Das Erlebnis und die
Dichtung* and *Das Leben Schleiermachers* are probably the
most inspired and instructive of his separate studies. A
valuable aid to the study of Dilthey is Misch's introduction
to *Gesammelte Schriften*, Bd. v.

BIBLIOGRAPHY

3. MAX WEBER, 1864–1920, born in Erfurt (Thüringen), for many years at Heidelberg, later at Munich.

WORKS

Gesammelte Aufsätze zur Religionssoziologie, 3 Bände, Tübingen, 1921 (containing in vol. 1 "Die protestantische Ethik und der Geist des Kapitalismus").
English translation: *The Protestant Ethic and the Spirit of Capitalism*; transl. by T. Parsons, with a Foreword by R. H. Tawney, London, 1930.
Gesammelte Aufsätze zur Sozial- und Wirtschaftsgeschichte, Tübingen.
Gesammelte Aufsätze zur Soziologie und Sozialpolitik, Tübingen.
Wirtschaft und Gesellschaft (Grundriss der Sozialökonomik, III. Abteilung), Tübingen, 1922.
Gesammelte Aufsätze zur Wissenschaftslehre, Tübingen, 1922.
Gesammelte Politische Schriften, München, 1921.
The two lectures "Wissenschaft als Beruf" and "Politik als Beruf" (reprinted in *Ges. Aufs. z. Wissenschaftslehre* and in *Gesammelte Politische Schriften* respectively) are obtainable in separate editions from Duncker und Humblot, München, 1919.

For a first acquaintance with Weber's thought the two lectures "Wissenschaft als Beruf" and "Politik als Beruf", given in the winter of 1918–19, are to be recommended. Those who are interested in him as a politician will go on to his *Gesammelte Politische Schriften*, a great part of which are concerned with War-time problems, but which include also his Inaugural Lecture on "Der Nationalstaat und die Volkswirtschaftspolitik" (1895) and a considerable number of letters on political subjects written to friends. As to his achievements as a scholar, his *Gesammelte Aufsätze zur Religionssoziologie*, especially that on "Die protestantische Ethik und der Geist des Kapitalismus", his essays on "Die sozialen Gründe des Untergangs der antiken Welt" (published in *Ges. Aufs. z. Sozial- und Wirtschaftsgeschichte*) and on "Die Börse" (published in *Ges. Aufs. z. Soziologie und Sozialpolitik*), further on "Die Objectivität sozialwissenschaftlicher und sozialpolitischer Erkenntnis", "Objective Möglichkeit und adäquate Verursachung in der historischen Kausalbetrachtung" and "Der Sinn der 'Wertfreiheit' der soziologischen und ökonomischen Wissenschaften" (all published in *Ges. Aufs. z. Wissenschaftslehre*), and finally his chief theoretical work, *Wirtschaft und Gesellschaft*, with its important methodological introduction are especially worth studying. For a fuller knowledge of his life, work and character the biography by his wife Marianne Weber (Tübingen, 1926) is indispensable. The force of his personality is brought out in the memorial address, delivered after his death by Jaspers (Tübingen, 1921), and the range and the significance of his work are discussed by the same author in a small book *Max Weber; Deutsches Wesen im politischen Denken, im Forschen und Philosophieren* (Oldenburg i. O., 1932).

Under the influence of Dilthey and Weber, but also under that of Lotze and of the Windelband-Rickert school ERNST TROELTSCH wrote his well-known works on "Die Soziallehren der christlichen Kirchen" (*Gesammelte Schriften*, Bd. I, Tübingen, 1919) and on "Der Historismus und seine Probleme" (*Gesammelte Schriften*, Bd. III, Tübingen, 1922).

BIBLIOGRAPHY

4. FRIEDRICH NIETZSCHE, 1844–1901, born at Röcken near Lützen (Thüringen), Professor of Classical Philology at Basel 1869–1879, outbreak of his mental disease at the end of 1888.

WORKS

Gesamtausgabe, in 19 Bänden, Leipzig, 1905 ff. (Abteilung I, Bd. 1–8, Werke. Abteilung II, Bd. 9–16, Nachlass. Abteilung III, Bd. 17–19, Philologica.)

Neue chronologisch geordnete Gesamtausgabe, Musarion Verlag, München, 1920 ff.
    English translation: *Complete Works*, 18 vols., ed. by O. Levy, London, 1909 ff.

Gesammelte Briefe, hrsg. von Elisabeth Foerster-Nietzsche, Berlin-Leipzig, 1900 ff., 5 Bände (especially interesting the correspondence with Erwin Rohde in the second, and with Jacob Burckhardt in the third volume).

Briefwechsel zwischen Nietzsche und Overbeck, hrsg. von R. Oehler und Bernoulli.
    English translation: *Selected Letters*, ed. by O. Levy, London, 1921.

In the work of Nietzsche four phases are to be distinguished. In the first (1869–76) he took as his standards the pre-Socratic culture of Greece, Schopenhauer and Wagner, and he regarded the artist and the philosopher as the culmination of all true civilisation; at this time, the *Birth of Tragedy* and the *Thoughts out of Season* were written. In the second (1876–81), independent of his former standards, he began critically to examine human life; this is the period of his philosophical explorations in which he could find no other way of expressing his thought than in aphorisms; to this period belong the works *Human, all-*

127

too-Human, The Dawn of the Day, and the first two volumes of *Joyful Wisdom*. In the third phase (August 1881 to the spring of 1885) he formulated poetically for himself his own philosophical task in symbols, such as "God is dead", pointing to his criticism of the highest Western values, "Superman", indicating his practical ideal and hope for the future after the dissolution of the former values, and "Eternal Return" which is the fullest expression of his acceptance without reserve of earthly reality as a whole; in these years the third and fourth volumes of *Joyful Wisdom* and *Thus spake Zarathustra* were composed; in the fourth (from the spring of 1885 to the end of 1888) he sought to elaborate his philosophical conception in separate preparatory investigations; this is the period of the prefaces to his earlier works, volume v of *Joyful Wisdom, Beyond Good and Evil, The Genealogy of Morals, The Twilight of the Idols, Case of Wagner, Will to Power* and *Ecce Homo*. A note of the spring of 1885, found among his papers: "Ich will reden und nicht mehr Zarathustra", marks the division between the two last periods.

Among his early works the *Birth of Tragedy* and, for his criticism of science, *The Use and Abuse of History*, for his conception of a philosopher, *Schopenhauer as Educator*, are especially noteworthy. Important among the later works are *The Genealogy of Morals* and *Beyond Good and Evil*, in which latter under the title "We Scholars" he discusses again the scientist and the philosopher, and under the title "What is noble" he gives expression to his conviction that nobility of character is an indispensable pre-requisite for a true philosopher. Moreover, in the *Will to Power*, and in fact in all of his works from *Human, all-too-Human* onwards, the reader will find many interesting and often stimulating ideas, provided that they are understood as having been formulated by a thinker who is in the one phase exploring and in the other elaborating; and the *Zarathustra* will receive justice when it is read as the poetical formulation of the thought of a man who has come in sight of his one philosophical task.

It is perhaps well to mention here that, among psychopathologists, the question has been seriously discussed whether certain changes in Nietzsche's style and thought as well as in his estimate of himself after August 1881 are not due to the first slight attacks of his mental disease; and it is assumed by almost all specialists that the works written in the second half of 1888 have been considerably affected by the excited condition immediately preceding the serious and permanently destructive attack.

5. SÖREN KIERKEGAARD, 1813–55, born in Copenhagen.

WORKS

Samlede Vaerker, 14 volumes, Copenhagen, 1900–06; new edition since 1920.

Papirer, Copenhagen, since 1909.

German translation of his works:

Gesammelte Werke, 12 Bände, hrsg. von Christoph Schrempf, Jena, 1909 ff. (Entweder-Oder, Bde I u. II. Furcht und Zittern; Wiederholung, Bd. III. Stadien auf dem Lesensweg, Bd. IV. Der Begriff der Angst, Bd. V. Philosophische Brocken; Unwissenschaftliche Nachschrift, Bde VI u. VII. Die Krankheit zum Tode, Bd. VIII. Einübung im Christentum, Bd. IX. Gesichtspunkt für meine Wirksamkeit als Schriftsteller, Bd. X. Zur Selbstprüfung der Gegenwart anempfohlen, Bd. XI. Der Augenblick, Bd. XII.)

CONTEMPORARY GERMAN PHILOSOPHY

Erbauliche Reden, 4 Bände, hrsg. von Christoph Schrempf, Jena, 1925 ff.

Religiöse Reden, hrsg. von Theodor Haecker, München, 1922.

Der Begriff des Auserwählten, hrsg. von Theodor Haecker, Innsbruck, 1926.

Kritik der Gegenwart, hrsg. von Theodor Haecker, Innsbruck, 1922.

Der Pfahl im Fleisch, hrsg. von Theodor Haecker, Innsbruck, 1922.

Die Tagebücher, 2 Bände, ausgewählt und übersetzt von Theodor Haecker, Innsbruck, 1923.

Kierkegaard's manner of writing and the variety of his works render it difficult to suggest a plan for the study of his philosophy. In the section devoted to him I endeavoured to give a first explanation which might be of use in the reading of "Entweder-Oder". In Germany "Der Begriff der Angst" and "Die Krankheit zum Tode" are the two books which have very deeply influenced readers of philosophy. Besides these, the "Unwissenschaftliche Nachschrift" is of great importance, especially because of its exposition of "Existenz" and "Existential Thinking", which includes the criticism of Hegel. An understanding of Kierkegaard would be further assisted by the reading of his *Tagebücher* as well as of Kierkegaard's own accounts of his work, given in the "Unwissenschaftliche Nachschrift" (*Ges. W*. Bd. vi, S. 324–70 and Bd. vii, S. 274–8) and especially in the "Gesichtspunkt für meine Wirksamkeit als Schriftsteller" (*Ges. W*. Bd. x, S. 1–100 and S. 157–70).

BIBLIOGRAPHY

6. KARL JASPERS, born 1883 in Oldenburg, Professor of Philosophy at Heidelberg.

WORKS

Allgemeine Psychopathologie, Berlin, 1913, 3. vermehrte und verbesserte Auflage, 1923.

Psychologie der Weltanschauungen, 3. Aufl., Berlin, 1925.

Strindberg und van Gogh, Versuch einer pathographischen Analyse unter vergleichender Heranziehung von Swedenborg und Hölderlin, Leipzig, 1922, 2. Aufl., 1926.

Die Idee der Universität, Berlin, 1923.

Die geistige Situation der Zeit (Sammlung Göschen), Berlin-Leipzig, 1931.
English translation: *Man in the Modern Age*, transl. by C. and E. Paul, London, 1933.

Philosophie, 3 Bände (I. Band: "Philosophische Weltorientierung"; II. Band: "Existenzerhellung"; III. Band: "Metaphysik"), Berlin, 1932.

Vernunft und Existenz, Fünf Vorlesungen, Groningen, 1935.

Jaspers' three principal works are: *Allgemeine Psychopathologie*, *Psychologie der Weltanschauungen* and *Philosophie*. The last-named work, discouraging as is its size, is the only source for a real knowledge of Jaspers' philosophical thought.

The study should begin with his explanations of "Ich selbst", "Kommunikation", "Geschichtlichkeit", "Grenzsituationen", "Absolutes Bewusstsein", "Unbedingte Handlungen" in the second volume, "Existenzerhellung", since this is not only the most creative part of his work, but it also contains the principles essential for a proper approach to the explanations in the other volumes. After this, his expositions in Chapters II, III and IV of the "Metaphysik" and his views on the essence of philosophy in the last three chapters of the "Philosophische Weltorientierung" are especially instructive.

Among his smaller works should be mentioned *Strindberg und van Gogh*, in which he endeavours to analyse the incomprehensible in mental disease in connection with the incomprehensible in genius; the *Idee der Universität* (1923), in which he, amidst the lack of fixed standards in post-war Germany, sought to remind his countrymen of the significance of a university; and the *Geistige Situation der Zeit* (1931), which he himself appears to regard as an introduction to his *Philosophie*, and which is much esteemed; it seems to me, however, that this work can be really understood only when one is already somewhat familiar with his philosophical thought. His newly published book, *Vernunft und Existenz*, offers in the first lecture an explanation of the historical significance of Kierkegaard and Nietzsche, develops, in the main section, some of the fundamental ideas of his philosophical Logic and characterises, in the last lecture, the new philosophising which Kierkegaard and Nietzsche have made possible.

7. MARTIN HEIDEGGER, born 1889 in Messkirch (Schwarzwald), Professor of Philosophy at Freiburg im Breisgau.

WORKS

Die Kategorien- und Bedeutungslehre des Duns Scotus, Tübingen, 1916.

Sein und Zeit, erste Hälfte, Halle, 1927 (first published in *Jahrbuch für Philosophie und phänomenologische Forschung*, Bd. VII).

Kant und das Problem der Metaphysik, Cohen, Bonn, 1929.

BIBLIOGRAPHY

Vom Wesen des Grundes, Halle, 1929 (first published in the *Festschrift für Husserl*).
Was ist Metaphysik? Cohen, Bonn, 1929.
Die Selbstbehauptung der deutschen Universität, Breslau, 1933.

His chief work is *Sein und Zeit*, Part 1. This alone can give an introduction into his distinctly original approach to philosophical problems. Two writings, *Kant und das Problem der Metaphysik* and *Vom Wesen des Grundes*, the first by expounding the advance beyond Greek philosophy towards a new metaphysics, made by Kant, the second by discussing one fundamental logical problem in its connection with metaphysics, supplement and explain the strictly systematic existential analyses in *Sein und Zeit*. On the other hand, his two well-known addresses, *Was ist Metaphysik?* and *Die Selbstbehauptung der deutschen Universität*, are in danger of being misinterpreted by those who have not an adequate understanding of his true philosophy.

PART 2

Works of other post-Hegelian German Philosophers

A. WORKS OF THE FIRST TWO PHILOSOPHICAL MOVEMENTS SINCE HEGEL

1. Attempts towards a philosophical synthesis of scientific results.

GUSTAV THEODOR FECHNER, 1801–87.
Die Tagesansicht gegenüber der Nachtansicht, Leipzig, 1879.

CONTEMPORARY GERMAN PHILOSOPHY

RUDOLF HERMANN LOTZE, 1817–81.
Mikrokosmos, 3 Bände, Leipzig, 1856–8, 1864.
English translation: *Microcosmos*, translated by E. Hamilton and E. E. C. Jones, 2 volumes, Edinburgh, 1885.
System der Philosophie (I. Teil: "Logik", neu herausgegeben von G. Misch, 1912, Leipzig; II. Teil: "Metaphysik", beide Teile).
English translation: *System of Philosophy*, translated by B. Bosanquet, Oxford, 1884.

EDUARD VON HARTMANN, 1842–1906.
Philosophie des Unbewussten, Berlin, 1869.

WILHELM WUNDT, 1832–1920.
System der Philosophie, 4. umgearbeitete Aufl., 2 Bände, 1919.

2. Epistemological enquiries and early researches into the foundations of the separate sciences.

ERNST COHEN, 1842–1918.
System der Philosophie (I. Teil: "Logik der reinen Erkenntnis"; II. Teil: "Ethik des reinen Willens"; III. Teil: "Aesthetik des reinen Gefühls", 2 Bände), Berlin, 1902–12.

WILHELM WINDELBAND, 1848–1915.
Präludien, 2 Bände, 4. erweiterte Aufl., Tübingen, 1911.

HEINRICH RICKERT, born 1863.
Der Gegenstand der Erkenntnis, 6. Aufl., Tübingen, 1928.
Die Grenzen der naturwissenschaftlichen Begriffsbildung, 5. Aufl., Freiburg, 1928.
Kulturwissenschaft und Naturwissenschaft, 6. u. 7. Aufl., Freiburg, 1926.
System der Philosophie (I. Teil: "Allgemeine Grundlegung der Philosophie"), Tübingen, 1921.

BIBLIOGRAPHY

HANS DRIESCH, born 1867.

Philosophie des Organischen, 2. verbesserte und teilweise umgearbeitete Aufl., Leipzig, 1921.

English edition: *The Science and Philosophy of the Organism*
(The Gifford Lectures delivered before the University of
Aberdeen in the year 1907), 2nd ed., London, 1929.

For the investigations into the principles and methods of
the separate sciences, undertaken by Dilthey, Weber and
Jaspers, see Part 1.

B. PHILOSOPHY OF LIFE

1. GEORG SIMMEL, 1858–1918

For his systematic view:
Lebensanschauung, 4 metaphysische Kapitel, München, 1918.
Hauptprobleme der Philosophie (Sammlung Göschen), Leipzig,
1910.

For his conception of biography:
Kant, 5. Aufl., Leipzig, 1921.
Schopenhauer und Nietzsche, Leipzig, 1906.
Goethe, Leipzig, 1913.
Rembrandt, Leipzig, 1916.

Other important philosophical works:
Probleme der Geschichtsphilosophie, 2. völlig veränderte Aufl.,
Leipzig, 1905.
Soziologie, Leipzig, 1908.
Philosophische Kultur, 2. vermehrte Aufl., Leipzig, 1919.
Zur Philosophie der Kunst, Potsdam, 1923.

135

CONTEMPORARY GERMAN PHILOSOPHY

2. MAX SCHELER, 1875–1928

Phenomenological and systematic works:

"Der Formalismus in der Ethik und die materiale Wertethik",
Halle, 1913–16 (published in *Jahrbuch für Philosophie und phänomenologische Forschung*, Bde I u. II).

Zur Phänomenologie und Theorie der Sympathiegefühle und von Liebe und Hass, Halle, 1913; 2. veränderte Auflage unter dem Titel *Wesen und Formen der Sympathie*, Bonn, 1923.

Die Wissensformen und die Gesellschaft, Leipzig, 1926.

Die Stellung des Menschen im Kosmos, Darmstadt, 1930.

Vom Umsturz der Werte (2. Aufl. der *Gesammelten Abhandlungen und Aufsätze*), 2 Bände, Leipzig, 1919.

Philosophische Weltanschauung, Bonn, 1929.

Schriften aus dem Nachlass, Bd. I, Berlin, 1933.

Characteristic examples of his power to express the tendencies of the time are:

Der Genius des Krieges und der deutsche Krieg, Leipzig, 1915.

Krieg und Aufbau, Leipzig, 1916.

Die Ursachen des Deutschenhasses, Leipzig, 1917.

Deutschlands Sendung und der katholische Gedanke, Berlin, 1918.

Vom Ewigen im Menschen, Bd. I: "Religiöse Erneuerung", Leipzig, 1921.

3. LUDWIG KLAGES, born 1872

Instructive studies of character-analysis and graphology are:

Ausdrucksbewegung und Gestaltungskraft, 4. Aufl., Leipzig, 1923.

Handschrift und Charakter, 12. Aufl., Leipzig, 1929.

Grundlagen der Charakterkunde, 6. Aufl., Leipzig, 1928.

A valuable study of mythology from a metaphysical point of view:

Vom kosmogonischen Eros, 3. Aufl., München, 1930.

His systematic work on metaphysics:

Der Geist als Widersacher der Seele, 3 Bände, Leipzig, 1929 ff.

BIBLIOGRAPHY

4. OSWALD SPENGLER, born 1880

Der Untergang des Abendlandes, 2 Bände, München, 1918–22.
    English translation: *The Decline of the West*, translated by
    C. F. Atkinson, London, 1926 f.
Der Mensch und die Technik, München, 1931.
    English translation: *Man and Technics*, translated by C. F.
    Atkinson, London, 1932.
Jahre der Entscheidung, München, 1933.
    English translation: *The Hour of Decision*, translated by C. F.
    Atkinson, London, 1934.

C. PRESENT ACADEMIC PHILOSOPHY

1. NICOLAI HARTMANN, born 1882

His most important systematic works from an ontological
point of view are:

Grundzüge einer Metaphysik der Erkenntnis, 2. Aufl., Berlin-
    Leipzig, 1925.
Ethik, Berlin-Leipzig, 1925.
    English translation: *Ethics*, 3 volumes, translated by S. Coit,
    London, 1932.
Das Problem des geistigen Seins, Berlin, 1933.

And newly published:

Zur Grundlegung der Ontologie, Berlin, 1935.

Among his historical works may be mentioned:

Philosophie des deutschen Idealismus (Bd. 1: "Fichte, Schelling
    und die deutsche Romantik"; Bd. 11: "Hegel"), Berlin-
    Leipzig, 1923–9.

2. Ernst Cassirer, born 1874

Systematic works:

Substanzbegriff und Funktionsbegriff, Berlin, 1910; 2. Aufl. 1923.
Philosophie der symbolischen Formen, 3 Bände, Berlin, 1923, 1924, 1929.

Historical works:

Das Erkenntnisproblem in der Philosophie und Wissenschaft der neueren Zeit, 3 Bände, Berlin, 1906, 1907, 1920.
Freiheit und Form. Studien zur deutschen Geistesgeschichte, Berlin, 1917.
Kants Leben und Lehre, Berlin, 1918.
Idee und Gestalt (essays on Goethe, Schiller, Hölderlin, Kleist), Berlin, 1921.
Individuum und Kosmos in der Philosophie der Renaissance, Leipzig, 1927.
Die Philosophie der Aufklärung, Tübingen, 1932.
Die platonische Renaissance in England und die Schule von Cambridge, Leipzig, 1932.

3. Phenomenological School

Earlier phenomenologists of realistic tendencies:

Alexander Pfänder, born 1870.
"Zur Psychologie der Gesinnungen", Halle, 1913–16 (published in *Jahrbuch für Philosophie und phänomenologische Forschung*, Bde I u. II).

His first phenomenological analysis (contemporaneous with that of Husserl) was:

Phänomenologie des Wollens, Leipzig, 1901.

Later works are:

Logik, Halle, 1921.
Psychologie des Menschen, Halle, 1933.

BIBLIOGRAPHY

MORITZ GEIGER, born 1880.
"Beiträge zur Phänomenologie des ästhetischen Genusses", Halle, 1913 (published in *Jahrbuch für Philosophie und phänomenologische Forschung*, Bd. I).

Particularly instructive among his later works are:
"Das Fragment über den Begriff des Unbewussten und die psychische Realität", Halle, 1921 (published in *Jahrbuch für Philosophie und phänomenologische Forschung*, Bd. IV).
Systematische Axiomatik der Euklidischen Geometrie, Augsburg, 1923.
Zugänge zur Aesthetik, Leipzig, 1928.
Die Wirklichkeit der Wissenschaften und die Metaphysik, Cohen, Bonn, 1930.

ADOLF REINACH, 1883–1916.
Gesammelte Schriften, Halle, 1921, hrsg. von H. Conrad-Martius.

From the realistic tendency Reinach developed a strictly ontological type of research which influenced a number of pupils including H. Conrad-Martius, A. Koyré, H. Lipps.

Among the early phenomenological researches WILHELM SCHAPP, *Beiträge zur Phänomenologie der Wahrnehmung*, Halle, 1910, is noteworthy.

MAX SCHELER, see under "B. Philosophy of Life".

MARTIN HEIDEGGER, see in Part I.

Of the younger phenomenologists influenced by Heidegger may be mentioned

OSKAR BECKER, born 1889.
"Mathematische Existenz", Halle, 1927 (first published in *Jahrbuch für Philosophie und phänomenologische Forschung*, Bd. VIII).

KARL LÖWITH, born 1897.
Das Individuum in der Rolle des Mitmenschen, München, 1928.

CONTEMPORARY GERMAN PHILOSOPHY

4. DILTHEY SCHOOL

GEORG MISCH, born 1878.

Geschichte der Autobiographie, Bd. I: "Das Altertum", Leipzig, 1907.

Vorbericht zu W. Dilthey's Gesammelte Schriften, Bd. v, Leipzig-Berlin, 1924.

Der Weg in die Philosophie, Berlin, 1926. (A comparative analysis of the development of the Indian, Chinese and the pre-Socratic Greek philosophy, based on a thorough study of the philosophical literature and undertaken for the purpose of understanding the essence and origin of philosophy.)

Lebensphilosophie und Phänomenologie. Eine Auseinandersetzung der Diltheyschen Richtung mit Heidegger und Husserl, Leipzig-Berlin, 1931.

HERMAN NOHL, born 1879.

Stil und Weltanschauung, Jena, 1920.

Pädagogische Aufsätze, 2. Aufl., Langensalza, 1930.

"Die Theorie der Bildung", "Die pädagogische Bewegung in Deutschland", "Pädagogische Menschenkunde". (Three articles, published in vols. I and II of *Handbuch der Pädagogik*, hrsg. von H. Nohl and L. Pallat), Langensalza, 1929 ff.

Die aesthetische Wirklichkeit, Frankfurt a. M., 1935.

EDUARD SPRANGER, born 1882.

Wilhelm von Humboldt und die Humanitätsidee, Berlin, 1909.

Lebensformen, 7. Aufl., Halle, 1930.

Psychologie des Jugendalters, 14. Aufl., Leipzig, 1931.

Kultur und Erziehung, 4. Aufl., Leipzig, 1928.

BERNHARD GROETHUYSEN, born 1880.

Die Entstehung der bürgerlichen Welt- und Lebensanschauung in Frankreich, 2 Bände, Halle, 1927–30.

BIBLIOGRAPHY

5. GESTALT THEORY

MAX WERTHEIMER, born 1880.

Über Schlussprozesse im produktiven Denken, Berlin, 1920.

Drei Abhandlungen zur Gestalttheorie, Erlangen, 1925.

WOLFGANG KÖHLER, born 1887.

Intelligenzprüfungen an Menschenaffen, 2. Aufl., Berlin, 1921.
  English translation: *The Mentality of Apes*, translated by E. Winter, 2nd ed., London, 1927.

Die physischen Gestalten in Ruhe und im stationären Zustand, Braunschweig, 1920.

Gestalt Psychology, London, 1930.

Psychologische Probleme, Berlin, 1933.

KURT KOFFKA, born 1886.

Die Grundlagen der psychischen Entwicklung, 2. Aufl., Osterwieck a. H., 1925.

6. GROUP OF SCIENTIFIC PHILOSOPHY

MORITZ SCHLICK, born 1882.

Allgemeine Erkenntnislehre, 2. Aufl., Berlin, 1925.

Naturphilosophie, published in *Lehrbuch der Philosophie*, Bd. II, hrsg. von M. Dessoir, Berlin, 1925.

RUDOLF CARNAP, born 1891.

Der logische Aufbau der Welt, Leipzig, 1928.

Abriss der Logistik, Wien, 1929.

"Logische Syntax der Sprache", Wien, 1934 (published in *Schriften zur wissenschaftlichen Weltauffassung*, Bd. VIII).

HANS REICHENBACH, born 1891.

Philosophie der Raum-Zeit-Lehre, Berlin, 1928.

Atom und Kosmos, Berlin, 1930.

INDEX

Adler, A., 89
Anaximander, 112
Aquinus, Th., 94, 111
Aristotle, 88, 94, 109, 111, 112, 113
Augustine, 75, 77, 94, 109, 111, 114

Bachofen, J. J., 72
Bacon, Fr., 120
v. Baer, K. E., 6
Barth, K., 73
Becker, O., 139
Bergson, H., 48, 94
Bleuler, E., 89
Boeckh, A., 7, 20
Brentano, F., xviii, 89, 123
Bruno, Giordano, 120
Bühler, Ch., 89
Bühler, K., 89
Burckhardt, J., 7, 8

Carnap, R., 93, 141
Carus, C. G., 6, 72
Cassirer, E., xviii, 88, **89–91**, 138
Cohen, E., **12–13**, 41, 89, 91, 94, 107, 134
Conrad-Martius, H., 139
Cuvier, G., 6

Darwin, Ch., 6
Descartes, R., 5, 6, 18, 90, 111, 113, 114, 120
Dilthey, W., xviii, xix, 13, 14, **20–6**, 26, 27, 41, 42–3, 45, 48, 58, 65, 66, 78, 84, 89, 91, **92**, 94, 97, 108, 109, 115, 116, **123–4**, 126

Dostoievsky, F. M., 75, 76
Driesch, H., 14, 94, 135
Duns Scotus, 94

Fechner, G. Th., **9–11**, 66, 93, 107, 133
Feuerbach, L., 74
Fichte, J. G., 3, 4, 11, 88, 104, 111
Freyer, H., 92
Freud, S., 70, 77, 89
v. Frisch, K., 89

Geiger, M., xii, 18, 20, 90, 91, 139
Gelb, A., 92
Geoffroy St.-Hilaire, Et., 6
George, St., 46, 67, 72
Goethe, J. W., 3, 4, 6
Grimm, F., 7, 20
Groos, K., 89
Groethuysen, B., 92, 140
Gundolf, F., 14

Haeckel, E., 6
Hamann, J. G., 3
v. Hartmann, Eduard, 6, **9–11**, 107, 134
Hartmann, Nicolai, xi, xii, xviii, 14, 88, **89–91**, 137
Hegel, G. W. F., xvi, xviii, 1, 3, 4, 7, 10, 11, 21, 24, 26, 45, 48, 62, 66, 67, 74, 84, 85, 86, 88, 89, 93, 94, 95, 105, 106, 111, 115, 117, 118, 130
Heidegger, M., xii, xviii, 19, 45, 55, 73, 77, 83, 87, 91, 93, 94, 97, **109–17**, 120, **132**

INDEX

Heimsoeth, H., 88
Heraclitus, 112
Herbart, J. F., 6
Herder, J. G., 3, 7, 89, 109
Hoffmann, E., 88
v. Humboldt, W., 4, 7
Hume, D., 6, 120
Husserl, E., xi, xviii, xix, 5, 14, 15-20, 21, 22, 23, 26, 27, 41, 43, 45, 48, 66, 91-2, 94, 97, 110, 121-3

Jaeger, W., 88
James, W., 69
Jaspers, K., xii, xviii, 13, 14, 26, 45, 55, 73, 77, 83, 87, 89, 90, 93, 94, 95-108, 109, 117, 120, 126, 131-2
Jung, C. G., 89

Kafka, G., 89
Kant, I., xvi, xvii, 3, 5, 12, 14, 21, 25, 52, 70, 85, 86, 94, 95, 100, 101, 104, 109, 111, 113, 115, 120, 133
Kastil, A., 123
Keyserling, Graf H., 68
Kierkegaard, S., xviii, 45, 46, 58, 72-86, 89, 94, 96, 97, 101, 102, 104, 109, 111, 115, 129-30, 132
Klages, L., 13, 55, 68, 70, 71-2, 77, 78, 90, 136
Klibansky, R., 88
Koffka, K., 89, 92, 141
Köhler, W., 89, 92, 141
Koyré, A., 139
Kraus, O., 123
Kretschmer, E., 89
Kroner, R., 88

Leibniz, G. W., 5, 6, 88, 105, 111, 120
Lessing, G. E., 3

Lipps, H., 139
Locke, J., 6, 120
Löwith, K., 139
Lotze, H., 9-11, 66, 93, 107, 126, 134
Luther, M., 77

Mann, Th., 46
Marty, A., 123
Marx, K., 7, 74
Meinong, A., 123
Mill, J. S., 15
Misch, G., xii, 88, 92, 123, 124, 140
Müller, J., 6
Müller, O., 7

Nelson, L., xviii
Newton, I., 4
Nicholas of Cusa, 88, 106
Niebuhr, B. G., 7
Nietzsche, Fr., xviii, 6, 33, 34, 36, 45, 46-67, 68, 69, 72, 75, 78, 84, 86, 88, 89, 96, 97, 98, 109, 127-9, 132
Nohl, H., 92, 140

Parmenides, 94, 109, 112
Pascal, Bl., 75
Pfänder, A., 18, 90, 91, 138
Plato, xii, 24, 52, 54, 101, 104, 106, 111, 112, 113

v. Ranke, L., 7, 20
Reichenbach, H., 93, 141
Reinach, A., 91, 139
Reinhardt, K., 88
Rickert, H., 13, 21, 108, 126, 134

Sachs, J., 6
v. Savigny, F. K., 7
Schapp, W., 139

INDEX

Scheler, M., xviii, 18, 20, 45, 48, 55, 68, **70–1**, 90, 91, 136
Schelling, F. W. J., 3, 4, 6, 10, 11, 74, 88, 105, 111
Schiller, Fr., 4
Schlegel, A. W., **7**
Schlegel, F., 7
Schleiermacher, F. E. D., 3, 4, 7, 11, 73
Schlick, M., 93, 141
Schmalenbach, H., xii, 88
Schopenhauer, A., 9, 10, 50, 56, 58, 62, 127
Simmel, G., xviii, 45, 48, 55, **68–70**, 78, 123, 135
Socrates, 24, 52, 64, 80, 111
Spengler, O., 68, **71**, 137
Spinoza, B., 104, 120
Spranger, E., 88, 89, 90, 92, 140

Steiner, R., 68
Stenzel, J., 88
Stern, W., 89
Stumpf, C., 123

Troeltsch, E., 23, 126

Wasmann, E., 89
Weber, Marianne, 126
Weber, Max, xii, xviii–xix, 8, 13, 14, **26–40**, 40, 41–2, 43, 45, 47, 48, 49, 94, 98, **125–6**
Weismann, A., 6
Wertheimer, M., 92, 141
Windelband, W., 13, 21, 94, 107, 126, 134
Wolf, F. A., 7
Wundt, W., **9–11**, 19, 93, 107, 134

For EU product safety concerns, contact us at Calle de José Abascal, 56–1°, 28003 Madrid, Spain or eugpsr@cambridge.org.

www.ingramcontent.com/pod-product-compliance
Ingram Content Group UK Ltd.
Pitfield, Milton Keynes, MK11 3LW, UK
UKHW020314140625
459647UK00018B/1875